KT-442-944

SONGS OF A SUN-LOVER

BY THE SAME AUTHOR

Verse

SONGS OF A SOURDOUGH
BALLADS OF A CHEECHAKO
RHYMES OF A ROLLING STONE
RHYMES OF A RED CROSS MAN
BALLADS OF A BOHEMIAN
BAR-ROOM BALLADS
COLLECTED VERSE

Novels

THE TRAIL OF '98
THE PRETENDER
THE POISONED PARADISE
THE ROUGHNECK
THE MASTER OF THE MICROBE
THE HOUSE OF FEAR

Miscellaneous

WHY NOT GROW YOUNG?

Autobiography

PLOUGHMAN OF THE MOON
HARPER OF HEAVEN

SONGS OF A SUN-LOVER

A Book of Light Verse

By

ROBERT SERVICE

ERNEST BENN LIMITED
LONDON

First Published 1949

Published by Ernest Benn Limited
Bouverie House, Fleet Street, London
Made and Printed in Great Britain
by The Stanhope Press, Ltd., Rochester

DEDICATION
TO
PROVENCE

I loved to toy with tuneful rhyme,
My fancies into verse to weave;
For as I walked my words would chime
So bell-like I could scarce believe;
My rhythms rippled like a brook,
My stanzas bloomed like blossoms gay:
And that is why I deem this book
    A verseman's holiday.

The palm-blades brindle in the blaze
Of sunsets splendouring the sea;
The gloaming is a lilac haze
That impish stars stab eagerly. . . .
O Land of Song! O golden clime!
O happy me, whose work is play!
Please take this tribute of my rhyme:
    A verseman's holiday.

CONTENTS

CONTENTS

CONTENTS

CONTENTS

LOWLY LAUREATE

O Sacred Muse, my lyre excuse!—
My verse is vagrant singing;
Rhyme I invoke for simple folk
Of penny-wise upbringing:
For Grannies grey to paste away
Within an album cover;
For maids in class to primly pass,
And lads to linger over.

I take the clay of every day
And mould it in my fashion;
I seek to trace the commonplace
With humour and compassion.
Of earth am I, and meekly try
To be supremely human:
To please, I plan, the little man,
And win the little woman.

No evil theme shall daunt my dream
Of fellow-love and pity;
I tune my lute to prostitute,
To priest I pipe my ditty.
Though gutter-grime be in my rhyme,
I bow to altars holy. . . .
Lord, humble me, so I may be
A Laureate of the Lowly.

MACTAVISH

I do not write for love of pelf,
Nor lust for phantom fame;
I do not rhyme to please myself,
Nor yet to win acclaim:
No, strange to say it is my plan,
What gifts I have, to lavish
Upon a simple working man,
　MACTAVISH.

For that's the rather smeary name,
Of dreary toil a hinter,
That heads the galley proofs that came
This morning from my printer;
My patient pencil much they need,
Yet how my eyes they ravish,
As at the top of each I read:
　MACTAVISH.

Who is this meek and modest man,
Who puffs no doubt a pipe,
And has my manuscript to scan,
And put in magic type?
Somehow I'm glad that he is not
Iberian or Slavish—
I hail him as a brother Scot,
　MACTAVISH.

I do not want to bore him with
My work, I make it snappy;
For even though his name were Smith,
I'd like him to be happy.
I hope, because I'm stumped for rhyme,
He will not think me knavish,
If I should call him just this time:
  MACTAYVISH.

Forgive me, Friend Mactavish, I
No doubt have cost you curses;
I'm sorry for you as you try
To put my type in verses;
And though new names I know you by,
When of new books creator,
I'll always look on you as my
  COLLABORATOR.

INSPIRATION

How often have I started out
With no thought in my noddle,
And wandered here and there about,
Where fancy bade me toddle;
Till feeling faunlike in my glee
I've voiced some gay distiches,
Returning joyfully to tea,
A poem in my britches.

A-squatting on a thymy slope
With vast of sky about me,
I've scribbled on an envelope
The rhymes the hills would shout me;
The couplets that the trees would call,
The lays the breezes proffered . . .
Oh no, I didn't *think* at all—
I took what Nature offered.

For that's the way you ought to write—
Without a trace of trouble;
Be super-charged with high delight
And let the words out-bubble;
Be voice of vale and wood and stream
Without design or proem:
Then rouse from out a golden dream
To find you've made a poem.

So I'll go forth with mind a blank,
And sea and sky will spell me;
And lolling on a thymy bank
I'll take down what they tell me;
As Mother Nature speaks to me
Her words I'll gaily docket,
So I'll come singing home to tea
A poem in my pocket.

BIRTHDAY
(16th January 1949)

I thank whatever gods may be
For all the happiness that's mine;
That I am festive, fit and free
To savour women, wit and wine;
That I my game of golf enjoy,
And have a formidable drive:
In short, that I'm a gay old boy
Though I be
        Seventy-and-five.

My daughter thinks, because I'm old
(I'm not a crock, when all is said),
I mustn't let my feet get cold,
And should wear woollen socks in bed;
A worsted night-cap too, forsooth!
To humour her I won't contrive:
A man is in his second youth
When he is
        Seventy-and-five.

At four-score years old age begins,
And not till then, I warn my wife;
At eighty I'll recant my sins,
And live a staid and sober life.
But meantime let me whoop it up,
And tell the world that I'm alive:
Fill to the brim the bubbly cup—
Here's health to
        Seventy-and-five!

THE BATTLE OF THE BULGE

This year an ocean trip I took, and as I am a Scot
And like to get my money's worth I never missed a meal.
In spite of Neptune's nastiness I ate an awful lot,
Yet felt as fit as if we sailed upon an even keel.
But now that I am home again I'm stricken with disgust;
How many pounds of fat I've gained I'd rather not
    divulge:
Well, anyway I mean to take this tummy down or bust,
So here I'm suet-strafing in the
                      Battle of the Bulge.

No more will sausage, bacon, eggs provide my breakfast
    fare;
On lobster I will never lunch, with mounds of *mayon-
naise*.
At tea I'll Spartanly eschew the chocolate *éclair*;
Roast duckling and *pêche melba* shall not consummate my
    days.
No more nocturnal ice-box raids, midnight spaghetti
    feeds;
On slabs of *pâté de foie gras* I vow I won't indulge:
Let bran and cottage cheese suffice my gastronomic needs,
And lettuce be my ally in the
                      Battle of the Bulge.

To hell with you, ignoble paunch, abhorrent in my sight
I gaze at your rotundity, and savage is my frown.
I'll rub you and I'll scrub you and I'll drub you day and
   night,
But by the gods of symmetry I swear I'll get you down
Your smooth and smug convexity, by heck! I wil
   subdue,
And when you tucker in again with joy will I refulge;
No longer of my toes will you obstruct my downward
   view . . .
With might and main I'll fight to gain the
                              Battle of the Bulge.

VANITY

My tangoing seemed to delight her;
With me it was love at first sight.
I mentioned that I was a writer;
She asked me: "What is it you write?"
"Oh, only best-sellers," I told her.
Their titles? . . . She shook her blonde head;
The atmosphere seemed to grow colder:
Not *one* of my books had she read.

Oh, she was a beauty ensnaring,
And I was an author of note;
But little I saw she'd be caring
If never a novel I wrote.
Alas for the caprice of Cupid!
Alack for the phantom of Fame!
I thought her just homely and stupid:
She didn't know even my *name*.

I saw her a score of years after;
She gushed as I took off my hat;
But inwardly loud was my laughter,
For she was enormously fat.
Thank heaven I'd not made *that* error;
I saw Love drive off in a hearse;
But I too retreated in terror . . .
She started to quote me my verse.

MY DENTIST

Sitting in the dentist's chair,
Wishing that I wasn't there,
To forget and pass the time
I have made this bit of rhyme.

I had a *rendez-vous* at ten;
I rushed to get in line,
But found a lot of dames and men
Had waited there since nine;
I stared at them, then in an hour
Was blandly ushered in;
But though my face was grim and sour
He met me with a grin.

He told me of his horse of blood,
And how it "also ran";
He plans to own a racing stud—
(He seems a wealthy man.)
And then he left me there until
I growled: "At any rate,
I hope he'll not charge in his bill
For all the time I wait."

His wife has sables on her back,
With jewels she's ablaze;
She drives a stately Cadillac,
And I'm the mug who pays:

At least I'm one of those who peer
With pessimistic gloom
At magazines of yester-year
In his damn waiting room.

I am a Christian Scientist;
I don't believe in pain;
My dentist has a powerful wrist,
He tries and tries in vain
To make me grunt or groan or squeal
With probe or rasp or drill. . . .
But oh, what agony I feel
When HE PRESENTS HIS BILL !

Sitting in the dental chair,
Don't you wish you weren't there:
Well, your cup of woe to fill,
Just think of his infernal bill.

CANINE CONVERSATION

If dogs could speak, O Mademoiselle,
What funny stories they could tell!
For instance, take your little "peke",
How awkward if the dear could speak!
How sad for you and all of us,
Who round you flutter, flirt and fuss:
Folks think you modest, mild and meek . . .
But would they—if Fi-fi could speak?

If dogs could tell, Ah Madame Rose,
What secrets could they not disclose!
If your pet poodle Angeline
Could hint one half of what she's seen,
Your reputation would, I fear,
As absolutely disappear
As would a snowball dropped in hell . . .
If Angeline could only tell.

If dogs could speak, how dangerous
It would be for a lot of us!
At what they see and what they hear
They wink an eye and wag an ear.
How fortunate for old and young
The darlings have a silent tongue!
We love them, but it's just as well
For all of us that—dogs can't tell.

POOCH

Nurse, won't you let him in?
He's barkin' an' scratchin' the door,
Makin' so dreffel a din
I jest can't sleep any more;
Out there in the dark an' the cold,
Hark to him scrape an' whine,
Breakin' his heart o' gold,
Poor little pooch o' mine.

Nurse, I was sat in ma seat
In front o' the barber shop,
When there he was lickin' ma feet
As if he would never stop;
Then all on a sudden I see
That dog-catcher moseyin' by:
"Whose mongrel is that?" says he;
"It's ma pedigree pup," says I.

Nurse, he was starved an' a-stray,
But his eyes was plumbful o' trust.
How could I turn him away?
I throwed him a bit o' a crust,
An' he choked as he gulped it up,
Then down at ma feet he curled:
Poor little pitiful pup!
Hadn't a friend in the world.

Nurse, I was friendless too,
So we was makin' a pair.
I'm black as a cast-off shoe,
But that li'le dog didn't care.
He loved me as much as though
Ma skin was pearly an' white:
Somehow dogs seem to know
When a man's heart's all right.

Nurse, we was thick as thieves;
Nothin' could pry us apart,
An' now to hear how he grieves
Is twistin' a knife in ma heart.
As I worked at ma shoe-shine stand
He'd watch me wi' eyes o' love,
A-wigglin' an' lickin' ma hand
Like I was a god above.

Nurse, I sure had no luck
That night o' the rain an' the fog;
There was that thunderin' truck,
And right in the way—ma dog.
Oh, I was a fool, I fear;
It's harder to think than to feel . . .
I dashed in, flung the pup clear,
But—I went under the wheel. . . .

Nurse, it's a-gittin' dark;
Guess ma time's about up:
Don't seem to hear him bark,
Poor, broken-hearted pup! . . .
Why, here he is, darn his skin!
Lickin' ma face once more:
How did the cuss git in?
Musta' busted the door.

God, I'm an ol' black coon,
But You ain't conscious o' race.
I gotta be goin' soon,
I'll be meetin' You face to face.
I'se been sinful, dice an' hooch,
But Lordy, before I die
I'se a-prayin': "Be good to ma pooch" . . .
That's all—little mut, good-bye.

BINGO

The daughter of the village Maire
Is very fresh and very fair,
    A dazzling eyeful;
She throws upon me such a spell
That though my love I dare not tell,
    My heart is sighful.
She has the cutest brown *caniche*,
The French for "poodle" on a leash,
    While I have Bingo;
A dog of doubtful pedigree,
Part pug or pom or chow maybe,
    But full of stingo.

The daughter of the village Maire
Would like to speak with me, I'll swear,
    In her sweet lingo;
But *parlez-vous* I find a bore,
For I am British to the core,
    And so is Bingo.
Yet just to-day as we passed by,
Our two dogs halted eye to eye,
    In friendly poses;
Oh, how I hope to-morrow they
Will wag their tails in merry play,
    And rub their noses.

.   .   .   .   .

The daughter of the village Maire
To-day gave me a frigid stare,
    My hopes are blighted.
I'll tell you how it came to pass . . .
Last evening in the Square, alas!
    My sweet I sighted;
And as she sauntered with her pet,
Her dainty, her adored Frolette,
    I cried: "By Jingo!"
Well, call it chance or call it fate,
I made a dash . . . Too late, too late!
    Oh, naughty Bingo!

Dear daughter of the village Maire,
That you'll forgive me, is my prayer
    And also Bingo.
You should have shielded your *caniche*;
You saw my dog strain on his leash
    And like a spring go.
They say that Love will find a way—
It definitely did, that day . . .
    Oh, canine noodles!
Now it is only left to me
To wonder —will your offspring be
    Poms, pugs or poodles?

TRIXIE

Dogs have a sense beyond our ken—
At least my little Trixie had:
Tail-wagging when I laughed, and when
I sighed, eyes luminously sad.
And if I planned to go away,
She'd know, oh, days and days before:
Aye, dogs I think are sometimes *fey*,
They seem to sense our fate in store.

Now take the case of old Tom Low;
With flowers each week he'd call on me.
Dear Trixie used to love him so,
With joyous jump upon his knee.
Yet when he wandered in one day,
Her hair grew sudden stark with dread;
She growled, she howled, she ran away . . .
Well, ten hours later Tom was dead.

Aye, dogs hear sounds we cannot hear,
And dogs see sights we cannot see;
And that is why I took the fear
That one day she would glare at me
As if a Shape cowered on my bed,
And with each hair on end she'd creep
Beneath the couch and whine with dread . . .
And so I've had her *put to sleep*.

Now Trixie's gone, the only one
Who loved me in my lonely life,
And here I wait, my race nigh run,
My ill too grievous for the knife.
My hand of ice she'll never lick,
My heedless mask she'll never see:
No heartbreak—just a needle prick. . . .
Oh, Doctor, do the same for me!

YELLOW

One pearly day of early May
I strolled upon the sand,
And saw, say half-a-mile away
A man with gun in hand;
A dog was cowering to his will,
As slow he sought to creep
Upon a dozen ducks so still
They seemed to be asleep.

When like a streak the dog dashed out,
The ducks flashed up in flight;
The fellow gave a savage shout
And cursed with all his might.
Then as I stood somewhat amazed
And gazed with eyes agog,
With bitter rage his gun he raised
And blazed and shot the dog.

You know how dogs can yelp with pain;
Its blood soaked in the sand,
And yet it crawled to him again
And tried to lick his hand.
"Forgive me, Lord, for what I've done,"
It seemed as if it said,
But once again he raised his gun:
This time he shot it—dead.

What could I do? What could I say?
'Twas such a lonely place.
Tongue-tied I saw him stride away,
I never saw his face.
I should have bawled the bastard out:
A yellow dog he slew;
But worse, he proved beyond a doubt
That—I was yellow too.

BOOK-BORROWER

I am a mild man, you'll agree,
    But red my rage is,
When folks who borrow books from me
    Turn down their pages.

Or when a chap a book I lend,
    And find he's loaned it
Without permission to a friend—
    As if *he* owned it.

But worst of all I hate those crooks
    (May hell-fires burn them!)
Who beg the loan of cherished books
    And don't return them.

My books are tendrils of myself
    No shears can sever . . .
May he who rapes one from its shelf
    Be damned forever.

BOOK-LOVER

I keep collecting books I know
I'll never, never read;
My wife and daughter tell me so,
And yet I never heed.
"Please make me," says some wistful tome,
"A wee bit of yourself."
And so I take my treasure home,
And tuck it in a shelf.

And now my very shelves complain;
They jam and over-spill.
They say: "Why don't you ease our strain?"
"Some day," I say, "I will."
So book by book they plead and sigh;
I pick and dip and scan;
Then put them back, distrest that I
Am such a busy man.

Now, there's my Boswell and my Sterne,
My Gibbon and Defoe;
To savour Swift I'll never learn,
Montaigne I may not know.
On Bacon I will never sup,
For Shakespeare I've no time;
Because I'm busy making up
These jingly bits of rhyme.

Chekov is caviare to me,
While Stendhal makes me snore;
Poor Proust is not my cup of tea,
And Balzac is a bore.
I have their books, I love their names,
And yet alas! they head,
With Lawrence, Joyce and Henry James,
My Roster of Unread.

I think it would be very well
If I commit a crime,
And get put in a prison cell
And not allowed to rhyme;
Yet given all these worthy books
According to my need,
I now caress with loving looks,
But never, never read.

MY LIBRARY

Like prim Professor of a College
I primed my shelves with books of knowledge;
And now I stand before them dumb,
Just like a child that sucks its thumb,
And stares forlorn and turns away,
With dolls or painted bricks to play.

They glour at me, my tomes of learning.
"You dolt!" they jibe; "you undiscerning
Moronic oaf, you made a fuss,
With highbrow swank selecting us;
Saying: 'I'll read you *all* some day'—
And now you yawn and turn away.

"Unwanted wait we with our store
Of facts and philosophic lore;
The scholarship of all the ages
Snug packed within our uncut pages;
The mystery of all mankind
In part revealed—but you are blind.

"You have no time to read, you tell us;
Oh, do not think that we are jealous
Of all the trash that wins your favour,
The flimsy fiction that you savour:
We only beg that sometimes you
Will spare us just an hour or two.

"For all the minds that went to make us
Are dust if folk like you forsake us,
And they can only live again
By virtue of your kindling brain;
In magic print they packed their best:
Come—try their wisdom to digest. . . ."

Said I: "Alas! I am not able;
I lay my cards upon the table,
And with deep shame and blame avow
I am too old to read you now;
So I will lock you in glass cases
And shun your sad, reproachful faces."

.   .   .   .   .   .

My library is noble planned,
Yet in it desolate I stand;
And though my thousand books I prize,
Feeling a witling in their eyes,
I turn from them in weariness
To wallow in the Daily Press.

For, oh, I never, never will
The noble field of knowledge till:
I pattern words with artful tricks,
As children play with painted bricks,
And realize with futile woe,
Nothing I know—*nor want to know.*

My library has windowed nooks;
And so I turn from arid books
To vastitude of sea and sky,
And like a child content am I
With peak and plain and brook and tree,
Crying: "Behold! the books for me:
Nature, be thou my Library!"

DUNCE

At school I never gained a prize,
Proving myself the model ass;
Yet how I watched with wistful eyes,
And cheered my mates who topped the class.
No envy in my heart I found,
Yet none was worthier to own
Those precious books in vellum bound,
Than I, a dreamer and a drone.

No prize at school I ever gained
(Shirking my studies, I suppose):
Yes, I remember being caned
For lack of love of Latin prose.
For algebra I won no praise,
In grammar I was far from bright:
Yet, oh, how Poetry would raise
In me a rapture of delight!

I never gained a prize at school;
The dullard's cap adorned my head;
My masters wrote me down a fool,
And yet—I'm sorry they are dead.
I'd like to go to them and say:
"Yours is indeed a tricky trade.
My honoured classmates, where are they?
Yet I, the dunce, brave books have made."

Oh, I am old and worn and grey,
And maybe have not long to live;
Yet 'tis my hope at some Prize Day
At my old school the Head will give
A tome or two of mine to crown
Some pupil's well-deserved success—
Proving a scapegrace and a clown
May win at last to worthiness.

STOWAWAY

We'd left the sea-gulls long behind,
And we were almost in mid-ocean;
The sky was soft and blue and kind,
The boat had scarcely any motion;
Except that songfully it sped,
And sheared the foam swift as an arrow . . .
When on my deck chair as I read
There fluttered down a city sparrow.

I stared with something of surprise;
The apparition mocked my seeming;
In fact I gently rubbed my eyes
And wondered if I were not dreaming.
It must, I mused, at Montreal
Have hopped abroad, somewhere to nestle,
And failed to hear the warning call
For visitors to leave the vessel.

Well, anyway a bird it was,
With winky eyes and wings a-twitter,
Unwise to Emigration Laws,
From Canada a hardy flitter;
And as it hopped about the deck
So happily I wondered whether
It wasn't scramming from Quebec
For London's mild and moister weather.

My rover's heart went out to it,
That vain, vivacious little devil;
And as I watched it hop and flit
I hoped it would not come to evil;
It planed above the plangent sea
(A foolish flight, I'd never risk it),
And then it circled back to me
And from my palm picked crumbs of biscuit.

Well, voyages come to an end
(We make them with that understanding);
One morn I missed my feathered friend,
And hope it made a happy landing.
Oh may she ever happy be
(If 'twas a "she"), with eggs to sit on,
And rest on our side of the sea,
A brave, brown, cheery, chirping Briton.

EUTHANASIA

A sea-gull with a broken wing
I found upon the kelp-strewn shore.
It sprawled and gasped; I sighed: "Poor thing!
I fear your flying days are o'er;
Sad victim of a savage gun,
So ends your soaring in the sun."

I only wanted to be kind;
Its icy legs I gently caught,
Thinking its fracture I might bind,
But fiercely in its fear it fought;
Till guessing that I meant no ill,
It glared and gaped, but lay quite still.

I took it home and gave it food,
And nursed its wing day after day.
Alas for my solicitude,
It would not eat, but pined away.
And so at last with tender hands
I took it to its native sands.

"I'll leave it where its kindred are,"
I thought, "And maybe they will cheer
And comfort it": I watched afar,
I saw them wheeling swiftly near. . . .
Awhile they hovered overhead,
Then darted down and—stabbed it dead.

When agonized is human breath,
And there's of living not a chance,
Could it not be that gentle death
Might mean divine deliverance?
Might it not seep into our skulls
To be as merciful as gulls?

FLIGHT

On silver sand where ripples curled
I counted sea-gulls seven;
Shy, secret, screened from all the world,
And innocent as heaven.
They did not of my nearness know,
For dawn was barely bright,
And they were still, like spots of snow
In that pale, pearly light.

Then one went forth unto the sea
That rippled up in gold,
And there were rubies flashing free
From out its wing-unfold;
It ducked and dived in pretty play,
The while the other six
So gravely sat it seemed that they
Were marvelled by its tricks.

Then with a sudden flurry each
Down-rushed to join its mate,
And in a flash that sickle beach
With rapture was elate.
With joy they pranked till everyone
Was diamonded with spray,
Then flicked with flame to greet the sun
They rose and winged away.

But with their going, oh, the surge
Of loss they left in me!
For in my heart was born the urge,
The passion to be free.
And where each dawn with terror brings
Some tale of bale and blight,
Who would not envy silver wings,
The sea-gull in its flight!

Let me not know the coils of woe
That chain this stricken earth;
Let me forget the fear and fret
That bind men from their birth;
Let me be one with wind and sun,
With earth and sky and sea. . . .
Oh, let me teach in living speech
God's glory—Liberty.

COURAGE

Ten little brown chicks scattered and scuffled,
Under the blue-berries hiding in fear;
Mother-grouse cackling, feathers all ruffled,
Dashed to defend them as we drew near.
Heart of a heroine, how I admired her!
Of such devotion great poets have sung;
Homes have been blest by the love that inspired her,
Risking her life for the sake of her young.

Ten little chicks on her valour reliant,
Peered with bright eyes from the bilberry spray;
Fiercely she faced us, dismayed but defiant,
Rushed at us bravely to scare us away.
Then my companion, a crazy young devil
(After, he told me he'd done it for fun)
Pretended to tremble, and raised his arm level,
And ere I could check him he blazed with his gun.

Headless she lay, from her neck the blood spouted,
And dappled her plumage, the poor, pretty thing!
Ten little chicks—oh, I know for I counted,
Came out and they tried to creep under her wing.
Sickened I said: "Here's an end to *my* killing;
I swear, nevermore bird or beast will I slay;
Starving I may be, but no more blood-spilling . . ."
That oath I have kept, and I keep it to-day.

WORMS

Worms finer for fishing you couldn't be wishing;
I delved them dismayed from the velvety sod;
The rich loam upturning I gathered them squirming,
Big, fat, gleamy earthworms, all ripe for my rod.
Thinks I, without waiting, my hook I'll be baiting,
And flip me a fish from the foam of the pool;
Then Mother beholding, came crying and scolding:
"You're late, ye young divil! Be off to the school."
So grabbing me bait-tin I dropped them fat worms in,
With gobs of green turf for their comfort and cheer;
And there, clean forgotten, no doubt dead and rotten,
I left them to languish for nigh on a year.

One day to be cleaning the byre I was meaning,
When seeing that old rusty can on a shelf,
Says I: "To my thinking, them worms must be stinking:
Begorrah! I'd better find out for myself."
So I opened the tin, held my nose and looked in;
And what did I see? Why, most nothing at all.
Just darkness and dank, and . . . a something that
    stank,
Tucked down in a corner, a greasy grey ball
My worms—no, not dead, but thin as a thread,
Each seemed to reproach me, protesting its worth:
So softly I took them and tenderly shook them
Back into the bosom of mothering earth.

I'm now in the City; 'tis grand, but I pity
The weariful wretches that crawl in its grime;
The dregs and the scum and the spawn of the slum,
And the poor little childer that's cradled in crime.
Sure I see them in terms of my pitiful worms,
Surviving despite desperation and doom,
And I wish I was God, with a smile and a nod
To set them all down in a valley of bloom,
Saying: "Let these rejoice with a wonderful voice
For mothering earth and for fathering sea,
And healing of sun, for each weariful one
Of these poor human worms is a wee bit of me. . . .
Let yours be the blame and yours be the shame:
What ye do unto them ye do also to ME."

WINDOW SHOPPER

I stood before a candy shop
Which with a Christmas radiance shone;
I saw my parents pass and stop
To grin at me and then go on.
The sweets were heaped in gleamy rows;
On each I feasted—what a game!
Against the glass with flatted nose,
Gulping my spittle as it came;
So still I stood, and stared and dreamed,
Savouring sweetness with my eyes,
Devouring dainties till it seemed
My candy shop was Paradise.

I had, I think, but five years old,
And though three-score and ten have passed,
I still recall the craintive cold,
The grimy street, the gritty blast;
And how I stared into that shop,
Its gifts so near and yet so far,
Of marzipan and toffee drop,
Of chocolate and walnut bar;
Imagining what I would buy
Amid delights so rich and rare . . .
The glass was misted with my sigh:
"If just one penny Pop could spare!"

And then when I went home to tea
Of bread with butter sparsely spread,
Oh, how my parents twitted me:
"You stood for full an hour," they said.
"We saw you as we passed again;
Your eyes upon the sweets were glued;
Your nose was flattened to the pane,
Like someone hypnotized you stood."
But when they laughed as at a joke,
A bitterness I could not stem
Within my little heart awoke. . . .
Oh, I have long forgiven them;
For though I know they did not own
Pennies to spare, they might, it seems
More understanding love have shown
More sympathy for those vain dreams,
Which make of me with wistful gaze
God's Window Shopper all my days.

MY HOLIDAY

I love the cheery bustle
Of children round the house,
The tidy maids a-hustle,
The chatter of my spouse;
The laughter and the singing,
The joy on every face:
With frequent laughter ringing,
Oh, Home's a happy place!

Aye, Home's a bit of heaven;
I love it every day;
My line-up of eleven
Combine to make it gay;
Yet when in June they're leaving
For Sandport by the sea,
By rights I should be grieving,
But gosh! I just feel *free*.

I'm left with parting kisses,
The guardian of the house;
The romp, it's true, one misses,
I'm quiet as a mouse.
In carpet slippers stealing
From room to room alone
I get the strangest feeling
The place is all my own.

It seems to nestle near me,
It whispers in my ear;
My books and pictures cheer me,
Hearth never was so dear.
In peace profound I lap me,
I take no stock of time,
And from the dreams that hap me,
I make (like this) a rhyme.

Oh, I'm ashamed of saying
(And think it's mean of me),
That when the kids are staying
At Sandport on the sea,
And I evoke them clearly
Disporting in the spray,
I love them still more dearly
Because . . . they're far away.

EYRIE

The little pink house is high on the hill
And my heart is not what it used to be;
It will kick up a fuss I know, but still
I must toil up that twisty trail to see
What that empty old house can mean to me.

For a Poet lived there for donkey's years,
A Poet of parts and founded fame.
He took to the bottle, it appears,
And hid up there to enjoy his shame . . .
Oh, no, I'll never betray his name.

Then gaily he drank himself to death,
But, oh, on the rarest of mellow wine;
An exquisite way to end one's breath—
Lachrimae Christi, I'd choose for mine,
To sip and souse in the sweet sunshine.

They say that poets are half divine;
I question if that is always true;
At least, our Poet was partly swine,
Drunk each day, with a drab or two,
Till Presto! he vanished from our view.

Maybe he was weary of woe and sin,
Or sick, and crawled like a dog to die;
Where the olives end and the pines begin,
He sought the peace of the sun and sky . . .
He would see no one, and I wonder why?

And so I must climb up, up some day
And try to picture my Poet there;
He sprawled on his rose-bowered porch, they sa
To smoke and fuddle and dream and stare
At the sapphire sea through the amber air.

He gave up the ghost with none to see;
In his bed, no doubt, though I'd fain surmise
It was yonder under the ilex tree,
Watching the sun in splendour rise,
With the glory of God-light in his eyes.

Well, he was a Lord of Radiant Rhyme;
His gift was godlike, one can't deny,
But he quit in the glory of his prime
As if he despised us—I wonder why?
As if he found, where yon mountains soar,
Far from men-folk and heaven-high,
Peace and Beauty forever more . . .
Peace and Beauty—Ah! so would I.

ESCAPE

Tell me, Tramp, where I may go
To be free from human woe;
Say where I may hope to find
Ease of heart and peace of mind;
Is there not some isle you know
Where I may leave Care behind?

So spoke one in sore distress,
And I answered softly: "Yes,
There's an isle so sweet and kind
So to clemency inclined,
So serene in loveliness
That the blind may lead the blind.

"Where there is no shade of fear,
For the sun shines all the year,
And there hangs on every tree
Fruit and food for you and me:
With each dawn so crystal clear
How like heaven earth can be!

"Where in mild and friendly clime
You will lose all count of time,
See the seasons blend in one,
Under sovereignty of sun;
Day with day resolve in rhyme,
Reveries and nothings done.

"You will mock the ocean roar,
Knowing you will evermore
Bide beside a lorn lagoon,
Listen to the ripples croon
On the muteness of the shore,
Silver-shattered in the moon.

"Come, let's quit this sorry strife,
Seek a sweeter, saner life,
Go so far, so very far
It just seems another star.
Go where joy and love are rife,
Go where peace and plenty are."

But he answered: "Brother, no,
To your isle I'll never go,
For the pity in my heart
Will not let me live apart
From God's world of want and woe:
I will stay and play my part,
Strive and suffer . . . Be it so."

PORTENT

Courage mes gars:
La guerre est proche.

I plant my little plot of beans,
I sit beneath my cyprus tree;
I do not know what trouble means,
I cultivate tranquillity . . .
But as to-day my walk I made
In all serenity and cheer,
I saw cut in an *agave* blade:
"Courage, my comrades, war is near!"

Seaward I went, my feet were slow,
Awhile I drowsed upon the shore;
And then I roused with fear for lo!
I saw six grisly ships of war.
A grim, grey line of might and dread
Against the skyline looming sheer:
With horror to myself I said:
"Courage, my comrades, war is near."

I saw my cottage on the hill
With rambling roses round the door;
It was so peaceful and so still
I sighed . . . and then it was no more.
A flash of flame, a rubble heap:
I cried aloud with woe and fear . . .
And woke myself from troubled sleep—
My home was safe, war was not near.

Oh, I am old, my step is frail,
My carcase bears a score of scars,
And as I climbed my homeward trail
Sadly I thought of other wars.
And when that *agave* leaf I saw
With vicious knife I made a blear
Of words clean-cut into the raw:
"Courage, my comrades, war is near."

Who put them there I do not know—
One of these rabid reds, no doubt;
But I for freedom struck my blow,
With bitter blade I scraped them out.
There now, said I, I will forget,
And smoke my pipe and drink my beer—
Yet in my mind these words were set:
"Courage, my comrades, war is near."

"Courage, my comrades, war is near."
I hear afar its hateful drums;
Its horrid din assails my ear:
I hope I die before it comes. . . .
Yet as into the town I go,
And listen to the rabble cheer,
I think with heart of weary woe:
War is not coming—WAR IS HERE.

NO MORE MUSIC

The porch was blazoned with geranium bloom;
Myrtle and jasmine meadows lit the lea;
With rose and violet the vale's perfume
Languished to where the hyacinthine sea
Dreamed tenderly . . . "And I must go," said he.

He spoke in that dim, ghostly voice of his:
"I was a singer; then the War . . . and GAS."
(I had to lean to him, no word to miss.)
"We bought this little *café* nigh to Grasse;
With sun and flowers my last few days will pass.

"And music too. I have my mandolin:
Say! Maybe you can strum on yon guitar . . .
Come on—we two will make melodious din,
While Madame sings to us behind the bar:
You'll see how sweet Italian folk-songs are."

So he would play and I would thrum the while;
I used to go there every lovely day;
His wife would listen with a sunny smile,
And when I left: "Please come again," she'd say.
"He seems quite sad when you have gone away."

Alas! I had to leave without good-bye,
And lived in sooty cities for a year.
Oh, how my heart ached for that happy sky!
Then, then one day my *café* I drew near—
God! it was strange how I was gripped with fear.

So still it was; I saw no mandolin,
No gay guitar with ribbons blue and red;
Then all in black, stone-faced the wife came in . . .
I did not ask; I looked, she shook her head:
"*La musique est fini*," was all she said.

TRANQUILLITY

This morning on my pensive walk
I saw a fisher on a rock,
Who watched his ruby float careen
In waters bluely crystalline,
While silver fishes nosed his bait,
Yet hesitated ere they ate.

Nearby I saw a mother mild
Who knitted by her naked child,
And watched him as he romped with glee,
In golden sand, in singing sea,
Her eyes so blissfully love-lit
She gazed and gazed and ceased to knit.

And then I watched a painter chap,
Grey-haired, a grandfather, mayhap,
Who daubed with delicate caress
As if in love with loveliness,
And looked at me with vague surmise,
The joy of beauty in his eyes.

Yet in my Morning Rag I read
Of paniked peoples, dark with dread,
Of flame and famine near and far,
Of revolution, pest and war;
The fall of this, the rise of that,
The writhing proletariat. . . .

I saw the fisher from his hook
Take off a shiny perch to cook;
The mother garbed her laughing boy,
And sang a silver lilt of joy;
The artist, packing up his paint,
Went home serenely as a saint.

The sky was gentleness and love,
The sea soft-crooning as a dove;
Peace reigned so brilliantly profound
In every sight, in every sound. . . .
Alas, what mockery for me!
Can peace be mine till Man be free?

PANTHEIST

Lolling on a bank of thyme
Drunk with Spring I made this rhyme. . . . .

Though peoples perish in defeat,
And races suffer to survive,
The sunshine never was so sweet,
So vast the joy to be alive;
The laughing leaves, the glowing grass
Proclaim how good it is to be;
The pines are lyric as I pass,
The hills hosannas sing to me.

Pink roses ring yon placid palm,
Soft shines the blossom of the peach;
The sapphire sea is satin calm,
With bell-like tinkle on the beach;
A lizard lazes in the sun,
A bee is bumbling to my hand;
Shy breezes whisper: "You are one
With us because you understand."

Yea, I am one with all I see,
With wind and wave, with pine and palm;
Their very elements in me
Are fused to make me what I am.

Through me their common life-stream flows,
And when I yield this human breath,
In leaf and blossom, bud and rose,
Live on I will . . . There is no Death.

Oh, let me flee from woeful things,
And listen to the linnet's song;
To solitude my spirit clings,
To sunny woodlands I belong.
O foolish men! Yourselves destroy,
But I from pain would win surcease. . . .
O Earth, grant me eternal joy!
O Nature—everlasting peace!

AMEN.

A VERSEMAN'S APOLOGY

Alas! I am only a rhymer,
I don't know the meaning of Art;
But I learned in my little school primer
To love Eugene Field and Bret Harte.
I hailed Hoosier Ryley with pleasure,
To John Hay I took off my hat:
These fellows were right to my measure,
And I've never gone higher than that.

The Classics! Well, most of them bore me,
The Moderns I don't understand;
But I keep Burns, my kinsman, before me,
And Kipling, my friend, is at hand.
They taught me my trade as I know it,
Yet though at their feet I have sat,
For God-sake don't call me a poet,
For I've never been guilty of that.

A rhyme-rustler, rugged and shameless,
A Bab Balladeer on the loose;
Of saccarine sonnets I'm blameless,
My model has been—Mother Goose.
And I fancy my grave-digger griping
As he gives my last lodging a pat:
"That guy wrote McGrew;
'Twas the best he could do" . . .
So I'll go to my Maker with that.

NO SOURDOUGH

To be a *bony feed* Sourdough
You must, by Yukon Law,
Have killed a moose,
And robbed a sluice,
AND BUNKED UP WITH A SQUAW. . . .

Alas! Sourdough I'll never be.
Oh, sad is my excuse:
My shooting's so damn bad, you see . . .
I've never killed a moose.

KATHLEEN

s the steamer *Alice May* that sailed the Yukon foam,
touched at every river camp from Dawson down to Nome.
s her builder, owner, pilot, Captain Silas Geer,
took her through the angry ice, the last boat of the year;
patched her cracks with gunny sacks and wound her pipes with wire,
cut the spruce upon the banks to feed her boiler fire;
headed her into the stream and bucked its mighty flow,
nosed her up the little creeks where no one else would go;
bragged she had so small a draft, if dew was on the grass,
gallant heart and half a start his little boat would pass.
ships might come and ships might go, but steady every year
Alice May would chug away with Skipper Silas Geer.

though Cap Geer had ne'er a fear the devil he could bilk,
wned a gastric ulcer and his grub was mostly milk.
lso owned a Jersey cow to furnish him the same,
oft and sleek and mild and meek, and Kathleen was her name.
as his source of nourishment he got to love her so
everywhere the Captain went the cow would also go;
though his sleeping quarters were ridiculously small,
pped a section of them off to make Kathleen a stall.
ery morn she'd wake him up with mellifluous moo,
he would pat her on the nose and go to wake the crew.

67

Then when he'd done his daily run and hitched on to the b
She'd breathe above his pillow till to soothing sleep he s
So up and down the river seeded sourdoughs would allo
They made a touching tableau, Captain Silas and his cow.

Now as the Captain puffed his pipe and Kathleen chewed
    cud,
There came to him a poetess, a Miss Belinda Budd.
"An epic I would write," said she, "about this mighty str
And from your gallant bark 'twould be romantic as a drea
Somewhat amazed the Captain gazed at her and shook his h
"I'm sorry, Miss, but we don't take *she* passengers," he sa
"My boat's a freighter, we have no accommodation space
For women-folk—my cabin is the only private place.
It's eight foot small from wall to wall, and I have, anyho
No room to spare, for half I share with Kathleen, that'
    cow."
The lady sighed, then soft replied: "I love your Yukon s
And for its sake your room I'll take, and put up with Kathle

Well, she was so dead set to go the Captain said: "By he
I like your spunk; you take my bunk and I'll camp on the d
So days went by then with a sigh she sought him out an
"Oh, Captain Geer, Kathleen's a dear, but does she ha
    moo?
In early morn like motor horn she bellows overhead,
While all the night without respite she snorts above my

ow it's true she dotes on you, your smile she seems to miss;
leans so near I live in fear my brow she'll try to kiss.
fond regard makes it *so* hard my Pegasus to spur. . . .
please be kind and try to find another place for her."

eft of cheer was Captain Geer; his face was glazed with
  gloom:
scratched his head: "There ain't," he said, "another inch
  of room.
h freight we're packed; it's stowed and stacked—why even
  on the deck.
re's seven salted sourdoughs and they're sleeping neck and
  neck.
sorry, Miss, that Kathleen's kiss has put your muse to
  flight;
lize her amber eyes abstract you when you write.
ed to love them orbs above a-shining down on me,
when she'd chew my whiskers you can't calculate my glee.
't at all poetical, but gosh! I guess your plight,
will try to plan what I can fix up for to-night."

s while upon her berth the wan and weary Author Budd
ailed her fate, Kathleen sedate above her chewed her cud,
as he sought with brain distraught a steady course to
  steer,
find a plan, a worried man was Captain Silas Geer.
n suddenly alert was he, he hollered to his mate:
Patsy, press our poetess to climb on deck and wait.

Hip-hip-hooray! Bid her be gay and never more despair:
My search is crowned—by heck! I've found an answer to
    prayer."

To Patsy's yell like glad gazelle came bounding Bardess Bu
No more forlorn, with hope new-born she faced the foam
    flood;
While down the stair with eager air was seen to disappear.
Like one inspired (by genius fired) exultant Captain Geer.
Then up he came with eye aflame and honest face aglow,
And oh, how loud he laughed, as proud he led her do
    below.
"Now you may write by day or night upon our Yukon sc
For I," he cried, "have clarified the problem of Kathleen.
I thought a lot, then like a shot the remedy I found:
I jest unhitched her rope and switched the loving crea
    round.
No more her moo will trouble you, you'll sleep right res
    now.
Look, Lady, look!—I'm giving you . . . *the tail end of the c*

THE YUKONER

He burned a hole in frozen muck,
He pierced the icy mould,
And there in six-foot dirt he struck
A sack or so of gold.

He burned holes in the Decalogue,
And then it came about,
For Fortune's just a lousy rogue,
His "pocket" petered out.

And lo! 'twas but a year all told,
When there in shadow grim,
In six feet deep of icy mould
They burned a hole for him.

MONTREAL MAREE

You've heard of Belching Billy, likewise known as Windy I
As punk a chunk of Yukon scum as ever robbed a sluice;
A satellite of Soapy Smith, a capper and a shill,
A slimy tribute-taker from the Ladies on the Loose.
But say, you never heard of how he aimed my gore to spil
(That big gorilla gunnin' for a little guy like me,)
A-howlin' like a malamute an' ravin' he would drill
Me full of holes and all because of Montreal Maree.

Now Spike Mahoney's Nugget Bar was stiff with roa
    drunks,
And I was driftin' lonesome-like, scarce knowin' what to
So come I joined a poker game and dropped a hundred plu
And bein' broke I begged of Spike to take my I.O.U.
Says he: "Me lad, I'll help ye out, but let me make this c
If you don't pay by New Year's day your wage I'll garnish
So I was broodin' when I heard a whisper in my ear:
"What ees zee trouble, leetle boy?" said Montreal Maree.

Now dance-hall gels is good and bad, but most is in betw
Yeh, some is scum and some is dumb, and some is jest pl
    cold;
But of straight-shootin' Dawson dames Maree was rated qu
As pretty as a pansy, wi' a heart o' Hunker gold.
And so although I didn't know her more than passin' by
I told how Spike would seek my Boss, and jobless I woul
She listened sympathetic-like: "Zut! Baby, don' you cry:
I lend to you zee hundred bucks," said Montreal Maree.

w though I zippered up my mug somehow the story spread
at I was playin' poker and my banker was Maree;
d when it got to Windy Bill, by Golly, he saw red,
d reachin' for his shootin' iron he started after me.
r he was batty for that babe and tried to fence her in,
d if a guy got in his way, say, he was set to kill;
fortified with barbwire hooch and wickeder than sin:
ll plug that piker full of lead," exploded Windy Bill.

at night, a hundred smackers saved, with joy I started out
seek my scented saviour in her cabin on the hill;
t barely had I paid my debt, when suddenly a shout . . .
eered from out the window, and behold! 'twas Windy Bill.
whooped and swooped and raved and waved his gun as he
drew near.
w he was kickin' in the door, no time was there to flee;
place to hide: my doom was sealed . . . then softly in my
ar:
uick! creep beneez my petticoat," said Montreal Maree.

pale as death I held my breath below that billowed skirt,
l as she sat I wondered at her voice so calm and clear;
ene and still she spoke to Bill like he was so much dirt
spdee de skunk! You jus' beeg drunk. You see no man is here,"
en Bill began to cuss and ran wild shootin' down the hill,
d all was hushed, and how I wished that bliss could ever be,
en up she rose in dainty pose beside the window sill:
e spill hees gun, run Baby, run," cried Montreal Maree.

I've heard it said that she got wed and made a wonder wife
I guess she did; that careless kid had mother in her heart.
But anyway I'll always say she saved my blasted life,
For other girls may come and go, and each may play th
  part:
But if I live a hundred years I'll not forget the thrill,
The rapture of that moment when I kissed a dimpled knee,
And safely mocked the murderous menace of Windy Bill,
Snug hid beneath the petticoat of Montreal Maree.

THE THREE BARES

tried to wash her garden slacks but couldn't get 'em clean
so she thought she'd soak 'em in a bucket o' benzine.
worked all right. She wrung 'em out then wondered what
e'd do
h all that bucket load of high explosive residue.
knew that it was dangerous to scatter it around,
Grandpa liked to throw his lighted matches on the ground.
ehow she didn't dare to pour it down the kitchen sink,
what the heck to do with it, poor Ma jest couldn't think.

n Nature seemed to give the clue, as down the garden lot
spied the edifice that graced a solitary spot,
ir Palace of Necessity, the family joy and pride,
hrined in morning-glory vine, with graded seats inside;
like that cabin Goldylocks found occupied by three,
in this case B-E A R was spelt B-A-R-E—
ny seat for Baby Bare, a medium for Ma,
ull-sized section sacred to the Bare of Grandpapa.

l, Ma was mighty glad to get that worry off her mind,
hefting up the bucket so combustibly inclined,
hurried down the garden to that refuge so discreet,
dumped the liquid menace safely through the *centre* seat.

t morning old Grandpa arose; he made a hearty meal,
sniffed the air and said: "By Gosh! how full of beans I feel.
ned if I ain't as fresh as paint; my joy will be complete
h jest a quiet session on the usual morning seat;
smoke me pipe an' meditate, an' maybe write a pome,
that's the time when bits o' rhyme gits jiggin' in me dome."

He sat down on that special seat slicked shiny by his age,
And looking like Walt Whitman, jest a silver-whiskered sa
He filled his corn-cob to the brim and tapped it snugly do
And chuckled: "Of a perfect day I reckon this the crown.'
He lit the weed, it soothed his need, it was so soft and sw
And then he dropped the lighted match *clean through the mi*
   seat.

His little grand-child Rosyleen cried from the kitchen doc
"Oh, Ma, come quick; there's sompin wrong; I heared a dr
   roar;
Oh, Ma, I see a sheet of flame; it's rising high and higher .
Oh, Mummy dear, I sadly fear our comfort-cot's caught fi

Poor Ma was thrilled with horror at them words o' Rosyl
She thought of Grandpa's matches and that bucket of benz
So down the garden geared on high, she ran with all her po
For regular was Grandpa, and she knew it was his hour.
Then graspin' gaspin' Rosyleen she peered into the fire,
A roarin' soarin' furnace now, perchance old Grandpa's pyre

But as them twain expressed their pain they heard a he
   cheer—
Behold the old rapscallion squattin' in the duck-pond nea
His silver whiskers singed away, a gosh-almighty wreck,
Wi' half a yard o' toilet seat entwined about his neck. . .

He cried: "Say, folks, oh, did ye hear the big blow-out I m
It scared me stiff—I hope you-uns was not too much afra
But now I best be crawlin' out o' this dog-gasted wet. .
For what I aim to figger out is—WHAT THE HECK I ET?''

MY MASTERS

Of Poetry I've been accused,
But much more often I have not;
Oh, I have been so much amused
By those who've put me on the spot,
And measured me by rules above
Those I observe with equal love.

An artisan of verse am I,
Of simple sense and humble tone;
My Thesaurus is handy by,
A rhyming lexicon I own;
Without them I am ill at ease—
What bards would use such aids as these?

Bad poets make good verse, they say;
The Great have not disdained to woo
The modest muse of every day;
Read Longfellow and Byron through,
The fabric test—much verse you'll see
Compared with what is poetry.

Small blame; one cannot always soar
To heights of hyaline sublime;
Melodious prose one must deplore,
And fetters of rebellious rhyme:
Keats, Browning—that's another tale,
But even Giants fall and fail.

I've worshipped Ryley, Harte and Field,
And though their minstrelsy I lack,
To them heart-homage here I yield,
And follow with my verseman's pack:
To them with gratitude I look,
For briefing me to make this book.

MY TYPEWRITER

I used to think a pot of ink
Held magic in its fluid,
And I would ply a *pen* when I
Was hoary as a Druid;
But as I scratch my silver thatch
My battered old Corona
Calls out to me as plaintively
As dying Desdemona.

"For old time's sake give me a break:
To you I've been as loyal
As ever could an Underwood,
Or Remington or Royal.
The globe we've spanned together and
Two million words, maybe,
For you I've tapped—it's time you rapped
A rhyme or two for me.

"I've seen you sit and smoke and spit
With expletives profane,
Then tear with rage the virgin page
I tendered you in vain.
I've watched you glare in dull despair
Through hours of brooding thought,
Then with a shout bang gaily out
The 'word unique' you sought.

"I've heard you groan and grunt and moan
That rhyme's a wretched fetter;
That after all you're just a small
Fat-headed verse-begetter;
You'd balance me upon your knee
Like any lady friend,
Then with a sigh you'd lay me by
For weeks and weeks on end.

"I've known when you were mighty blue
And hammered me till dawn,
Dire poverty! But I would be
The last thing you would pawn.
Days debt-accurst! Then at its worst
The sky, behold, would clear;
A poem sold, the garret cold
Would leap to light and cheer.

"You've toted me by shore and sea
From Mexico to Maine;
From Old Cathay to Mandalay,
From Samarkand to Spain.
You've thumped me in the battle's din
And pounded me in peace;
By air and land you've lugged me and
Your shabby old valise.

"But now my keys no more with ease
To your *two* fingers yield;
With years of use my joints are loose,
With wear of flood and field.
And even you are slipping too;
You're puffy, stiff and grey:
Old Sport, we're done, our race is run—
Why not call it a day?"

.   .   .   .   .

Why not? You've been, poor old machine!
My tried and faithful friend.
With fingertip your keys I'll flip
Serenely to the end.
For even though you're stiff and slow,
No other will I buy,
And though each word be wan and blurred
I'll tap you till I die.

THE LIVING DEAD

Since I have come to years sedate
I see with more and more acumen
The bitter irony of Fate,
The vanity of all things human.
Why, just to-day some fellow said,
As I surveyed Fame's outer portal:
"By gad! I thought that you were dead."
Poor me, who dreamed to be immortal!

But that's the way with many men
Whose name one fancied time-defying;
We thought that they were dust, and then
We found them living by their dying.
Like dogs we penmen have our day,
To brief best-sellerdom elected;
And then, "thumbs down", we slink away
And die forgotten and neglected.

Ah well, my lyric fling I've had;
A thousand bits of verse I've minted;
And some, alas! were very bad,
And some, alack! were best unprinted.
But if I've made my muse a bawd
(Since I am earthy as a ditch is),
I'll answer humbly to my God:
Most men at times have toyed with bitches.

Yes, I have played with Lady Rhyme,
And had a long and lovely innings;
And when the Umpire calls my time
I'll blandly quit and take my winnings.
I'll hie me to some Sleepydale,
And feed the ducks and pat the poodles,
And prime my paunch with cakes and ale,
And blether with the village noodles.

And then some day you'll idly scan
The Times obituary column,
And say: "Dear me, the poor old man!"
And for a moment you'll look solemn.
"So all this time he's been alive—
In realms of rhyme a second-rater . . .
But gad! to live to ninety-five:
Let's toast his ghost—a sherry, waiter!"

HOBO

A father's pride I used to know,
A mother's love was mine;
For swinish husks I let them go,
And bedded with the swine.
Since then I've come on evil days
And most of life is hell;
But even swine have winsome ways
When once you know them well.

One time I guessed I'd cease to roam,
And greet the folks again;
And so I rode the rods to home
And through the window pane
I saw them weary, worn and grey . . .
I gazed from garden gloom,
And like sweet, shiny saints were they
In that sweet, shiny room.

D'ye think I hollered out: "Hullo!"
The prodigal to play,
And eat the fatted calf? Ah no,
I cursed and ran away.
My eyes were blears of whisky tears
As to a pub I ran:
But once at least I beat the beast
And proved myself a man.

Oh, some day I am going back,
But I'll have gold galore;
I'll wear a suit of sober black
And knock upon the door.
I'll tell them how I've made a stake,
We'll have the grandest time. . . .
"Say, Mister, give a guy a break:
For Crissake, spare a dime."

DRIFTER

God gave you guts: don't let Him down;
Brace up, be worthy of His giving.
The road's a rut, the sky's a frown;
I know you're plumb fed up with living.
Fate birches you, and wry the rod . . .
Snap out, you fool! Don't let down God.

Oh, yes, you're on misfortune's shift,
And weary is the row you're hoeing;
You have no home, you drift and drift,
Seems folks don't care the way you're going . . .
Well, make them care—you're not afraid:
Step on the gas—you'll make the grade.

Believe that God has faith in you,
In you His loving light is shining;
All of you that is fine and true
Is part of Him, so quit your whining . . .
Buck up, son, for your Maker's sake:
Don't let Him down—give God a break.

HOT DIGITTY DOG

Hot digitty dog! Now, ain't it queer,
I've been abroad for over a year;
Seen a helluva lot since then,
Killed, I reckon, a dozen men;
Six was doubtful, but six was sure,
Three in Normandy, three in the Ruhr.
Four I got with a hand grenade,
Two I shot in a midnight raid:
Oh, I ain't sorry, except perhaps
To think that my jerries wasn't japs.

Hot digitty dog! Now ain't it tough;
I oughta be handed hero stuff—
Bands and banquets, and flags and flowers,
Speeches, peaches, confetti showers;
"Welcome back to the old home town,
Colour Sergeant Josephus Brown.
Fought like a tiger, one of our best,
Medals and ribands on his chest.
Cheers for a warrior, fresh from the fight . . ."
Sure I'd 'a got 'em—had I been *white*.

Hot digitty dog! It's jist too bad,
Gittin' home an' nobody glad;
Sneakin' into the Owl Drug Store,
Nobody knowin' me any more;

Admirin' my uniform fine and fit—
Say, I've certainly changed a bit
From the lanky lad who used to croon
To a battered banjo in Shay's Saloon;
From the no-good nigger who runned away
After stickin' his knife into ol' man Shay.

They'd a lynched me, for he was white,
But he raped my sister one Sunday night;
So I did what a proper man should do,
And I sunk his body deep in the slough.
Oh, he taunted me to my dark disgrace,
Called me nigger, spat in my face;
So I buried my jack-knife in his heart,
Laughin' to see the hot blood start;
Laughin' still, though it's long ago,
And nobody's ever a-gonna know.

Nobody's ever a-gonna tell
How Ol' Man Shay went straight to hell;
Nobody's gonna make me confess—
And what is a killin' more or less.
My skin may be black, but by Christ! I fight;
I've slain a dozen, and each was white,
And none of 'em ever did me no harm,
And my conscience is clear—I've no alarm:
So I'll go where I sank Ol' Man Shay in the bog,
And spit in the water . . . *Hot digitty dog!*

OLD ED

Our cowman, old Ed, hadn't much in his head,
And lots of folks thought him a witling;
But he wasn't a fool, for he always kept cool,
And his sole recreation was whittling.
When I'd spill him my woes (infantile, I suppose),
He'd harken and whittle and whittle;
Then when I had done, turn his quid and say: "Son,
Ye're a-drownin' yerself in yer spittle."

He's gone to his grave, but the counsel he gave
I've proved in predicaments trying;
When I got in a stew, feeling ever so blue,
My failures and faults magnifying,
I'd think of old Ed as he sniffed and he said:
"Shaw! *them* things don't matter a tittle.
Ye darned little cuss, why make such a fuss?
Ye're a-drownin' yerself in yer spittle."

When you're tangled with care till you're up in the air,
And worry and fear have you quaking,
When each tiny trouble seems bigger than double,
Till mountains of mole-hills you're making;
Go easy, my friend, things click in the end,
But maybe 'twill help you a little,
If you take Ed's advice (though it may not *sound* nice):
"Don't be drownin' yerself in yer spittle."

SCHIZOPHRENIC

Each morning as I catch my bus,
A-fearing I'll be late,
I think: there are in all of us
Two folks quite separate;
As one I greet the office staff
With grim, official mien;
The other's when I belly-laugh,
And Home Sweet Home's the scene.

I've half a hundred men to boss,
And take my job to heart;
You'll never find me at a loss,
So well I play my part.
My voice is hard, my eye is cold,
My mouth is grimly set;
They all consider me, I'm told,
A "bloody martinet."

But when I reach my home at night
I'm happy as a boy;
My kiddies kiss me with delight,
And dance a jig of joy.
I slip into my oldest clothes,
My lines of care uncrease;
I mow the lawn, unhook the hose,
And glow with garden peace.

It's then I wonder which I am,
The boss with hard-boiled eye,
Or just the gay don't-care-a-damn
Go-lucky garden guy?
Am I the starchy front who rants
As round his weight he throws,
Or just old Pop with patchy pants,
Who sings and sniffs a rose?

BABETTE

My Lady is dancing so lightly,
The belle of the Embassy Ball;
I lied as I kissed her politely,
And hurried away from it all.
I'm taxiing up to Montmartre,
With never a pang of regret,
To toy for awhile with the garter
Of her whom I know as Babette.

My Lady's an exquisite creature,
As rare as a queen on a throne;
She's faultless in form and in feature,
But oh, she is cold as a stone.
And so from her presence I hurry,
Her iciness quick to forget
In sensuous joy as I bury
My face in the breast of Babette.

She's only a flower of the pavement;
With Paris and Spring in her eyes;
Yet I who foresaw what the grave meant
Of passion behold with surprise,
When she greets me as gay as a linnet,
Afar from life's fever and fret,
I'm twenty years younger the minute
I enter the room of Babette.

The poor little supper she offers
Is more than a banquet to me;
A diffident *bif-tik* she proffers,
Pommes frit and a morsel of *Brie*;
We finish with coffee and kisses,
Then sit on the sofa and pet . . .
At the Embassy *Mumm* never misses,
But *pinard's* my drink with Babette.

Somehow and somewhere to my thinking,
There's a bit of *apache* in us all;
In *bistros* I'd rather be drinking,
Than dance at the Embassy Ball.
How often I feel I would barter
My place in the social set,
To roam in a moonlit Montmartre,
Alone with my little Babette.

I'm no longer young and I'm greying;
I'm tailored, top-hatted, kid-gloved,
And though in dark ways I be straying,
It's heaven to love and be loved;
The passion of youth to re-capture, . . .
My Lady's perfection and yet
When I kiss her I think of the rapture
I find in the charms of Babette—
Entwined in the arms of Babette.

NO LILIES FOR LISETTE

Said the Door: "She came in
With no shadow of sin;
Turned the key in the lock,
Slipped out of her frock,
The robe she liked best
When for supper she dressed.
Then a letter she tore . . .
What a wan look she wore!"
    Said the Door.

Said the Chair: "She sat down
With a pitiful frown,
And then (oh, it's queer)
Just one lonely tear
Rolled down her pale cheek.
How I hoped she would speak
As she let down her hair,"
    Said the Chair.

Said the Glass: "Then she gazed
Into me like one dazed;
As with delicate grace
She made up her face,
Her cheeks and her lips
With rose finger-tips,
So lovely—alas!
Then she *turned on the gas*,"
    Said the Glass.

Said the Bed: "Down she lay
In a weariful way,
Like an innocent child,
To her fate reconciled;
Hands clasped to her breast,
In prayer or in rest:
'Dear Mother,' she said,
Then pillowed her head,"
    Said the Bed.

Said the Room: "Then the gleam
Of the moon like a dream,
Soft silvered my space,
And it fell on her face
That was never so sweet
As her heart ceased to beat . . .
Then the moon fled and gloom
Fell like funeral plume,"
    Said the Room.

"Just a whore,"
Said the Door;
"Yet so fair,"
Said the Chair;
"Frail, alas!"
Said the Glass;
"Now she's dead,"
Said the Bed;
"Sorry doom,"
Said the Room. . . .

Then they all,
Floor and wall,
Quiet grew,
Ceiling too;
Like a tomb
Was the room;
With hushed breath
Hailing Death:
Soul's release,
Silence, Peace.

THE CHRISTMAS TREE

the dank and damp of an alley cold,
y the Christmas tree that hadn't been sold;
a shopman dourly thrown outside,
ith the ruck and rubble of Christmas-tide;
odden deep in the muck and mire,
worthy even to feed a fire. . . .
I stooped and salvaged that tarnished tree,
d this is the story it told to me:

Iy Mother was Queen of the forest glade,
d proudly I prospered in her shade;
r she said to me: 'When I am dead,
u will be monarch in my stead,
d reign, as I, for a hundred years,
ower of triumph amid your peers.
en I crash in storm I will yield you space;
n, you will worthily take my place.'

o I grew in grace like a happy child,
the heart of the forest free and wild;
d the moss and the ferns were all about,
d the craintive mice crept in and out;
d a wood-dove swung on my highest twig,
d a chipmunk chattered: 'So big! So big!'
d a shy fawn nibbled a tender shoot,
d a rabbit nestled under my root. . . .
, I was happy in rain and shine
I thought of the destiny that was mine!

Then a man with an axe came cruising by
And I knew that my fate was to fall and die.

"With a hundred others he packed me tight,
And we drove to a magic city of light,
To an avenue lined with Christmas trees,
And I thought: may be I'll be one of these,
Tinselled with silver and tricked with gold,
A lovely sight for a child to behold;
A-glitter with lights of every hue,
Ruby and emerald, orange and blue,
And kiddies dancing, with shrieks of glee—
One might fare worse than a Christmas tree.

"So they stood me up with a hundred more
In the blaze of a big department store;
But I thought of the forest dark and still,
And the dew and the snow and the heat and the chil.
And the soft chinook and the summer breeze,
And the dappled deer and the birds and the bees. . .
I was so homesick I wanted to cry,
But patient I waited for someone to buy.
And some said 'Too big,' and some 'Too small',
While some passed on saying nothing at all.
Then a little boy cried: 'Ma, buy that one,'
But she shook her head: 'Too dear, my son.'
So the evening came, when they closed the store,
And I was left on the littered floor,
A tree unwanted, despised, unsold,
Thrown out at last in the alley, cold."

hen I said: "Don't sorrow; at least you'll be
bright and beautiful New Year's tree,
ll shimmer and glimmer and glow and gleam,
radiant sight like a fairy dream.
or there is a little child I know,
ho lives in poverty, want and woe;
ho lies abed from morn to night,
nd never has known an hour's delight. . . ."

I stood the tree at the foot of her bed:
anta's a little late," I said.
oor old chap! Snowbound on the way,
t he's here at last, so let's be gay."
en she woke from sleep and she saw you there,
d her eyes were love and her lips were prayer.
d her thin little arms were stretched to you
ith a yearning joy that they never knew.
e woke from the darkest dark to see
ke a heavenly vision, that Christmas Tree.

r mother despaired and feared the end,
t from that day she began to mend,
play, to sing, to laugh with glee. . . .
ss you, O little Christmas Tree!
u died, but your life was not in vain:
u helped a child to forget her pain,
d let hope live in our hearts again.

WHITE CHRISTMAS

My folks think I'm a serving maid
Each time I visit home;
They do not dream I ply a trade
As old as Greece or Rome;
For if they found I'd fouled their name
And was not white as snow,
I'm sure that they would die of shame . . .
Please God, they'll never know.

I clean the paint from off my face,
In sober black I dress;
Of coquetry I leave no trace
To give them vague distress;
And though it causes me a pang
To play such sorry tricks,
About my neck I meekly hang
A silver crucifix.

And so with humble step I go
Just like a child again,
To greet their Christmas candle-glow,
A soul without a stain;
So well I play my contrite part
I make myself believe
There's not a stain within my heart
On Holy Christmas Eve.

With double natures we are vext,
And as we feel, we are;
A saint one day, a sinner next,
A red light or a star;
A prostitute or proselyte,
And in each part sincere:
So I become a vestal white
One week in every year.

For this I say without demur
From out life's lurid lore,
Each righteous woman has in her
A tincture of the whore;
While every harpy of the night,
As I have learned too well,
Holds in her heart a heaven-light
To ransom her from hell.

So I'll go home and sweep and dust;
I'll make the kitchen fire,
And be of model daughters just
The best they could desire,
I'll fondle them and cook their food,
And Mother dear will say:
"Thank God! my darling is as good
As when she went away."

But after New Year's Day I'll fill
My bag and though they grieve,
I'll bid them both good-bye until
Another Christmas Eve;
And then . . . a knock upon the door:
I'll find them waiting there,
And angel-like I'll come once more
In answer to their prayer.

Then Lo! one night when candle-light
Gleams mystic on the snow,
And music swells of Christmas bells,
I'll come, no more to go:
The old folks need my love and care,
Their gold shall gild my dross,
And evermore my breast shall bear
My little silver cross.

REVERENCE

I saw the Greatest Man on Earth,
Aye, saw him with my proper eyes.
A loin-cloth spanned his proper girth,
But he was naked otherwise,
Excepting for a grey sombrero;
And when his domelike head he bared,
With reverence I stared and stared,
As mummified as any Pharaoh.

He leaned upon a little cane,
A big cigar was in his mouth;
Through spectacles of yellow stain
He gazed and gazed towards the South;
And then he dived into the sea,
As if to Corsica to swim,
His side stroke was so strong and free
I could not help but envy him.

A fitter man than I, I said,
Although his age is more than mine;
And I was strangely comforted
To see him battle in the brine
Thought I: We have no cause for sorrow;
For one so dynamic to-day
Will gird him for the future fray
And lead us lion-like to-morrow.

The Greatest Man in all the world
Lay lazying like you or me,
Within a flimsy bathrobe curled
Upon a mattress by the sea:
He reached to pat a *tou-tou's* nose,
And scratched his torso now and then,
And scribbled with a fountain pen
What I assumed was jewelled prose.

And then methought he looked at me,
And hailed me with a gesture grand;
His fingers made the letter "V",
So I, too, went to raise my hand;—
When nigh to me the barman glided
With liquid gold, and then I knew
He merely called for cock-tails two,
And so abjectly I subsided.

Yet I have had my moment's glory,
A-squatting nigh that Mighty Tory,
Proud Hero of our Island Story.

EXTERNALISM

The Greatest Writer of to-day
(With Maupassant I almost set him)
Said to me in a weary way,
The last occasion that I met him:
"Old chap, this world is more and more
Becoming bourgeois, *blasé*, blousy:
Thank God I've lived so long before
It got so definitely lousy."

Said I: "Old Chap, I don't agree.
Why should one so dispraise the present?
For gainful guys like you and me,
It still can be extremely pleasant.
Have we not Woman, Wine and Song—
A gleeful trio to my thinking;
So blithely we can get along
With laughing, loving, eating, drinking."

Said he: "Dear Boy, it may be so,
But I'm fed up with war and worry;
I would escape this world of woe,
Of wrath and wrong, of hate and hurry.
I fain would gain the peace of mind
Of Lamas on Thibetan highlands,
Or maybe sanctuary find
With beach-combers on coral islands."

Said I: "Dear Boy, don't go so far:
Just live a life of simple being;
Forgetting all the ills that are,
Be satisfied with hearing, seeing.

The sense of smell and taste and touch
Can bring you bliss in ample measure:
If only you don't *think* too much,
Your programme can be packed with pleasure.

"But do not try to probe below
This fairy film of Nature's screening;
Look on it as a surface show,
Without a purpose or a meaning.
Take no account of social strife,
And dread no coming cataclysm:
Let your philosophy of life
Be what I call: EXTERNALISM.

"The moon shines down with borrowed light,
So savants say—I do not doubt it.
Suffice its silver trance my sight,
That's all I want to know about it.
A fig for science—'how' and 'why'
Distract me in my happy dreaming:
Through line and form and colour I
Am all content with outward seeming. . . ."

The Greatest Writer of to-day
(I would have loved to call him Willie),
Looked wry at me and went his way—
I think he thought me rather silly.
Maybe I am, but I insist
My point of view will take some beating:
Don't mock this old Externalist—
The pudding's proof is in the eating.

PEDLAR

Pedlar's coming down the street,
Housewives beat a swift retreat.
Don't you answer to the bell;
Heedless what she has to sell.
Latch the door—Oh, do not hide:
Just discreetly go inside.
We must hang a board, I fear:
PEDLARS NOT PERMITTED HERE.

I'm trying to sell what nobody wants to buy;
They turn me away, but still I try and try.
My arms are aching and my feet are sore;
Heartsick and worn I drag from door to door.
I ring bells, meekly knock, hold out my tray,
But no one answers, so I go away.
I am so weary; oh, I want to cry,
Trying to sell what no one wants to buy.

I do not blame them. Maybe in their place
I'd slam the door shut in a pedlar's face.
I do not know; perhaps I'd raise their hopes
By looking at their pens and envelopes,
Their pins and needles, pencils, spools of thread,
Cheap tawdry stuff, before I shake my head
And go back to my cosy kitchen nook
Without another thought or backward look.
I would not see their pain nor hear their sigh,
Trying to sell what no one wants to buy.

I know I am a nuisance. I can see
They only buy because they pity me.
They may . . . I've had a cottage of my own,
A husband, children—now I am alone,
Friendless in all the world. The bitter years
Have crushed me, robbed me of my dears.
All, all I've lost, my only wish to die,
Selling my trash that no one wants to buy.

Pedlar's beating a retreat—
Poor old thing, her face is sweet,
Her figure frail, her hair snow-white;
Dogone it! Every door's shut tight. . . .
"Say, Ma, how much for all you've got?
Hell, here's ten bucks . . . I'll take the lot.
Go, get yourself a proper feed,
A little of the rest you need.
I've got a mother looks like you—
I'd hate her doing what you do. . . .
No, don't get sloppy, can the mush,
Praying for me—all that slush;
But please don't come again this way,
Ten bucks is all I draw a day."

WALLFLOWER

Till midnight her needle she plied
To finish her pretty pink dress;
"Oh, bless you, my darling," she sighed;
"I hope you will be a success."
As she entered the Oddfellows' Hall
With the shy thrill of maiden romance
She felt like the belle of the Ball,
But . . . nobody asked her to dance.

Her programme was clutched in her hand;
Her smile was a tiny bit wan;
She listened, applauding the band,
Pretending she *liked* to look on.
Each girl had her favourite swain,
She watched them retreat and advance;
She waited and waited in vain,
But nobody asked her to dance.

Said Mother to me: "You'll agree
That any young girl who wears specs,
However so clever she be,
Is lacking in glamour of sex."
Said I: "There is one by the wall
Who doesn't seem having a chance.
She's ready to weep—Dash it all,
I'm going to ask her to dance."

I caught her just slipping away
So quietly no one would know;
But bravely she tried to seem gay,
Though her heart might be aching with woe.
Poor kid! She looked only sixteen,
And she gave me a half frightened glance
When I bowed as if she were a Queen,
And I begged: "May I please have this dance?"

She gave me her card: what a bluff!
She'd written "Sir G." and "Sir G."
So I cut out that Galahad stuff,
And I scribbled "M.E". and "M.E.";
She looked so forlorn and so frail,
Submitting like one in a trance,
So I acted the conquering male,
And guided her into the dance.

Then lo! to my joy and surprise
Her waltzing I found was divine;
And she took those damn specs from her eyes,
And behold, they were jewels a-shine;
No lipstick nor rouge she had on,
But no powder and paint could enhance
On her cheeks the twin roses that shone
As I had with her dance after dance.

Then all of a sudden I knew
As we waltzed and reversed round the hall
That all eyes were watching us two,
And that she was the Belle of the Ball.
The fellows came buzzing like bees,
With swagger and posture and prance,
But her programme was full of "M.E."'s,
So she couldn't afford them a dance.

Said Mother: "You've been a nice boy,
But had a good time, I suppose.
You've filled that poor kid's heart with joy,
From now she'll have plenty of beaus." . . .
So fellows, please listen to me:
Don't look at a wallflower askance;
If a girl sitting lonely you see,
Just bow, smile and beg for a dance.

STAMP COLLECTOR

My worldly wealth I hoard in albums three,
My life collection of rare postage stamps;
My room is cold and bare as you can see,
My coat is old and shabby as a tramp's;
Yet more to me than balances in banks,
My albums three are worth a million francs.

I keep them in that box beside my bed,
For who would dream such treasures it could hold;
But every day I take them out and spread
Each page, to gloat like miser o'er his gold:
Dearer to me than could be child or wife,
I would defend them with my very life.

They *are* my very life, for every night
Over my catalogues I pore and pore;
I recognize rare items with delight,
Nothing I read but philatelic lore;
And when some specimen of choice I buy,
In all the world there's none more glad than I.

Behold my gem, my British penny black;
To pay its price I starved myself a year;
And many a night my dinner I would lack,
But when I bought it, oh, what radiant cheer!
Hitler made war that day—I did not care,
So long as my collection he would spare.

Look—my triangular Cape of Good Hope.
To purchase it I had to sell my car.
Now in my pocket for some *sous* I grope
To pay my omnibus when home is far,
And I am cold and hungry and footsore,
In haste to add some beauty to my store.

This very day, ah, what a joy was mine,
When in a dingy dealer's shop I found
This *franc* vermillion, eighteen forty-nine . . .
How painfully my heart began to pound!
(It's weak, they say), I paid the modest price
And tremblingly I vanished in a trice.

But oh, my dream is that some day of days,
I might discover a Mauritius blue,
Poking among the stamp-bins of the *quais*;
Who knows! They say there are but two;
Yet if a third one I should ever spy,
I think—God help me! I should faint and die. . . .

Poor Monsieur Pons, he's cold and dead,
One of those stamp collecting cranks,
His garret hold no crust of bread,
But albums worth a million francs.
On them his income he would spend,
By philatelic frenzy driven:
What did it profit in the end. . . .
You can't take stamps to Heaven.

OLD TROUPER

I was Mojeska's leading man
And famous parts I used to play,
But now I do the best I can
To earn my bread from day to day;
Here in this Burg of Breaking Hearts,
Where one wins as a thousand fail,
I play a score of scurvy parts
Till Time writes Finis to my tale.

My wife is dead, my daughters wed,
With heaps of trouble of their own;
And though I hold aloft my head
I'm humble, scared and all alone . . .
To-night I burn each photograph,
Each record of my former fame,
And oh, how bitterly I laugh
And feed them to the hungry flame!

Behold how handsome I was then—
What glowing eye, what noble mien;
I towered above my fellow men,
And proudly strode the painted scene.
Ah, Vanity! What fools are we,
With empty ends and foolish aims . . .
There now, I fling with savage glee
My *David Garrick* to the flames.

"Is this a dagger that I see":
Oh, how I used to love that speech;
We were old-fashioned—"hams" maybe,
Yet we Young Arrogance could teach.
"Out, out brief candle!" There are gone
My *Lear*, my *Hamlet* and *Macbeth*;
And now by ashes cold and wan
I wait my cue, my prompter Death.

This life of ours is just a play;
Its end is fashioned from the start;
Fate writes each word we have to say,
And puppet-like we strut our part.
Once I wore laurels on my brow,
But now I wait, a sorry clown,
To make my furtive, farewell bow . . .
Haste Time! Oh, ring the Curtain down.

SENTIMENTAL SHARK

Give me a cabin in the woods
Where not a human soul intrudes;
Where I can sit beside a stream
Beneath a balsam bough and dream,
And every morning see arise
The sun like bird of paradise;
Then go down to the creek and fish
A speckled trout for breakfast dish,
And fry it at an ember fire—
Ah! there's the life of my desire.

Alas! I'm tied to Wall Street where
They reckon me a millionaire,
And sometimes in a day alone
I gain a fortune o'er the 'phone.
Yet I to be a man was made,
And here I ply this sorry trade
Of Company manipulation,
Of selling short and stock inflation:
I whom God meant to rope a steer,
Fate made a Wall Street buccaneer.

Old Timer, how I envy you
Who do the things I long to do.
Oh, I would swap you all my riches
To step into your buckskin britches.
Your ragged shirt and rugged health

I'd take in trade for all my wealth.
Then shorn of fortune you would see
How drunk with freedom I would be;
I'd kick so hard, I'd kick so high,
I'd kick the moon clean from the sky.

Aye, gold to me is less than brass,
And jewels mean no more than glass.
My gold is sunshine and my gems
The glint of dew on grassy stems . . .
Yet though I hate my guts it's true
Time sorta makes you used to you;
And so I will not gripe too much
Because I have the Midas touch,
But doodle on my swivel chair,
Resigned to be a millionaire.

PULLMAN PORTER

The porter in the Pullman car
Was charming, as they sometimes are.
He scanned my baggage tags: "Are you
The man who wrote of Lady Lou?"
When I said "yes" he made a fuss—
Oh, he was most assiduous;
And I was pleased to think that he
Enjoyed my brand of poetry.

He was forever at my call,
So when we got to Montreal
And he had brushed me off, I said:
"I'm glad my poems you have read.
I feel quite flattered, I confess,
And if you give me your address
I'll send you (autographed, of course)
One of my little books of verse."

He smiled—his teeth were white as milk;
He spoke—his voice was soft as silk.
I recognized, despite his skin,
The perfect gentleman within.
Then courteously he made reply:
"I thank you kindly, Sir, but I
With many other cherished tome
Have all your books of verse at home.

"When I was quite a little boy
I used to savour them with joy;
And now my daughter, aged three,
Can tell the tale of Sam McGee;
While Tom, my son, that's only two
Has heard the yarn of Dan McGrew. . . .
Don't think your stuff I'm not applaudin'—
My taste is Eliot and Auden."

So as we gravely bade adieu
I felt quite snubbed—and so would you.
And yet I shook him by the hand,
Impressed that he could understand
The works of those two tops I mention,
So far beyond *my* comprehension—
A humble bard of boys and barmen,
Disdained, alas! by Pullman carmen.

THE LOCKET

From out her shabby rain-coat pocket
The little Jew girl in the train
Produced a dinted silver locket
With pasted in it portraits twain.
"These are my parents, sir," she said;
"Or were, for now I fear they're dead.

"I know to Belsen they were sent;
I never heard of them again.
So many were like that—they went,
Our woeful quest was all in vain.
I was in London with a friend,
Or I, too, would have shared their end.

"They could have got away, I'm told,
And joined me here in Marylebone,
But Grannie was so sick and old,
They could not leave her there alone.
When they were seized she cried and cried:
Thank God! 'twas in her *bed* she died.

"How did *they* die? I cannot bear
To think of that—it crazes me.
My mother was so sweet, so fair;
My father handsome as you see . . .
I'm sure no daughter ever had
More lovely parents . . . Yes, it's sad.

"But for their loss I shall not grieve;
I'll hug the hope they still survive;
Oh, I must make myself believe
Somehow, somewhere they're still alive. . . .

"Well, that's my only souvenir,
A locket stained with many a tear."

For supper we had curried tripe.
I washed the dishes, wound the clock;
Then for awhile I smoked my pipe—
Puff! Puff! We had no word of talk.
The Missis sewed—a sober pair;
Says I at last: "I need some air."

I don't know why I acted so;
I had no thought, no plot, no plan.
I did not really mean to go—
I'm such a docile little man;
But suddenly I felt that I
Must change my life or I would die.

A sign I saw: A ROOM TO LET.
It had a musty, dusty smell;
It gloated gloom, it growled and yet
Somehow I felt I liked it well.
I paid the rent a month ahead:
That night I *smoked my pipe in bed*.

From out my world I disappeared;
My walk and talk changed over-night.
I bought black glasses, grew a beard—
Abysmally I dropped from sight;
Old Tax Collector, Mister Smith
Became a memory, a myth.

I see my wife in widow's weeds;
She's gained in weight since I have gone.
My pension serves her modest needs,
She keeps the old apartment on;
And living just a block away
I meet her nearly every day.

I hope she doesn't mourn too much;
She has a sad and worried look.
One day we passed and chanced to touch,
But as with sudden fear I shook,
So blankly in my face she peered,
I had to chuckle in my beard.

Oh, comfort is a blessed thing,
But forty years of it I had.
I never drank the wine of Spring,
No moon has ever made me mad.
I never clutched the skirts of Chance
Nor daftly dallied with Romance.

And that is why I seek to save
My soul before it is too late,
To put between me and the grave
A few years of fantastic fate:
I've won to happiness because
I've killed the man that once I was.

I've murdered Income Taxer Smith,
And now I'm Johnny Jones to you.
I have no home, no kin, no kith,
I do the things I want to do.
No matter though I've not a friend,
I've won to freedom in the end.

Bohemian born, I guess, was I;
And should my wife her widowhood
By wedlock end I will not sigh,
But pack my grip and go for good,
To live in lands where laws are lax,
And innocent of Income Tax.

EQUALITY

The Elders of the Tribe were grouped
And squatted in the Council Cave;
They seemed to be extremely pooped,
And some were grim, but all were grave:
The subject of their big To-do
Was axe-man Chow, the son of Choo.

Then up spoke Tribal Wiseman Waw:
"Brothers, to-day I talk to grieve:
As an upholder of the Law
You know how deeply we believe
In Liberty, Fraternity,
And likewise in Equality.

"A chipper of the flint am I;
I make the weapons that you use,
And though to hunt I never try,
To bow to hunters I refuse:
But stalwart Chow, the son of Choo
Is equal to us any two.

"He is the warrior supreme,
The Super caveman, one might say;
The pride of youth, the maiden's dream,
And in the chase the first to slay.
Where we are stunted he is tall:
In short, a menace to us all.

"He struts with throwing stone and spear;
And is he not the first to wear
Around his waist with bully leer
The pelt of wolf and baby bear!
Admitting that he made the kill,
Why should he so *exploit* his skill?

"Comrades, grave counsel we must take,
And as he struts with jest and jibe,
Let us act swiftly lest he make
Himself Dictator of our Tribe:
The Gods have built him on *their* plan:
Let us reduce him to a man."

And so they seized him in the night,
And on the sacrificial stone
The axe-men of the Tribe did smite,
Until one limb he ceased to own.
There! They had equalized the odds,
Foiling unfairness of the Gods.

So Chow has lost his throwing arm,
And goes around like every one;
No longer does he threaten harm,
And tribal justice has been done.
For men are equal, let us seek
To grade the Strong down to the weak.

FLIES

I never kill a fly because
I think that what we have of laws
To regulate and civilize
Our daily life—we owe to flies.

Apropos, I'll tell you of Choo, the spouse
Of the head of the hunters, Wung;
Such a beautiful cave they had for a house,
And a brood of a dozen young.
And Wung would start by the dawn's red light
On the trailing of bird or beast,
And crawl back tired on the brink of night
With food for another feast.

Then the young would dance in their naked glee,
And Choo would fuel the fire;
Fur and feather, how good to see,
And to gorge to heart's desire!
Flesh of rabbit and goose and deer,
With fang-like teeth they tore,
And laughed with faces a bloody smear,
And *flung their bones on the floor.*

But with morning bright the flies would come,
Clouding into the cave;
You could hardly hear for their noisy hum,
They were big and black and brave.

Darkling the day with gust of greed
They'd swarm in the warm sunrise
On the litter of offal and bones to feed—
A million or so of flies.

Now flies were the wife of Wung's despair;
They would sting and buzz and bite,
And as her only attire was hair
She would itch from morn to night:
But as one day she scratched her hide,
A thought there came to Choo:
"If I were to throw the bones outside,
The flies would go there too."

That spark in a well-nigh monkey mind,
Nay, do not laugh to scorn;
For there in the thought of Choo you'll find
Was the sense of Order born;
As she flung the offal far and wide,
And the fly-cloud followed fast,
Battening on the bones outside
The cave was clear at last.

And Wung was pleased when he came at night,
For the air was clean and sweet,
And the cave-kids danced in the gay firelight,
And fed on the new-killed meat;

But the children Choo would chide and boss,
For her cleanly floor was her pride,
And even the baby was taught to toss
His bit of a bone outside.

Then the cave crones came and some admired,
But others were envious;
And they said: "She swanks, she makes us tired
With her complex modern fuss."
However, most of the tribe complied,
Though tradition dourly dies,
And a few Conservatives crossly cried:
"We'll keep our bones and our flies."

So Reformer Choo was much revered
And to all she said: "You see
How my hearth is clean and my floor is cleared,
And there ain't no flies on me" . . .
And that was how it all began,
Through horror of muck and mess,
Even in prehistoric Man,
LAW, ORDER and CLEANLINESS.

*And that is why I never kill
A fly, no matter how obscene;
For I believe in God's good will:
He gave us vermin to make us clean.*

RHYME-SMITH

Oh, I was born a lyric babe
(That last word is a bore—
It's only rhyme is "astrolabe",
Whose meaning I ignore.)
From cradlehood I lisped in numbers,
Made jingles even in my slumbers.
Said Ma: "He'll be a bard, I know it."
Said Pa: "Let's hope he will outgrow it."

Alas! I never did, and so
A dreamer and a drone was I,
Who persevered in want and woe
His misery to versify.
Yea, I was doomed to be a failure
(Old Browning rhymes that last with "pale lure"):
And even starving in the gutter,
My macaronics I would utter.

Then in a poor, cheap book I crammed,
And to the public maw I tossed
My bitter Dirges of the Damned,
My biting Lyrics of the Lost.
"Let carping critic flay and flout
My Ditties of the Down and Out—
"There now," said I, "I've done with verse,
My love, my weakness and my curse."

Then lo! (As I would fain believe,
Before they crown, the Fates would shame us)
I went to sleep one bitter eve,
And woke to find that I was famous. . . .
And so the sunny sequels were a
Gay villa on the Riviera,
A bank account, a limousine, a
Life patterned *dolce e divina*.

Oh, yes, my lyric flight is flighty;
My muse is much more mite than mighty:
But poetry has been my friend,
And rhyming's saved me in the end.

THE ORDINARY MAN

If you and I should chance to meet,
I guess you wouldn't care;
I'm sure you'd pass me in the street
As if I wasn't there;
You'd never look me in the face,
My modest mug to scan,
Because I'm just a commonplace
   And Ordinary Man.

But then, it may be, you are too
A guy of every day,
Who does the job he's told to do
And takes the wife his pay;
Who makes a home and kids his care,
And works with pick or pen. . . .
Why, Pal, I guess we're just a pair
   Of Ordinary Men.

We plug away and make no fuss,
Our feats are never crowned;
And yet it's common coves like us
Who make the world go round.
And as we steer a steady course
By God's predestined plan,
Hats off to that almighty Force:
   THE ORDINARY MAN.

MY BOSS

My Boss keeps sporty girls, they say;
His belly's big with cheer.
He squanders in a single day
What I make in a year.
For I must toil with bloody sweat,
And body bent and scarred,
While my whole life-gain he could bet
Upon a single card.

My Boss is big and I am small;
I slave to keep him rich.
He'd look at me like scum and call
Me something of a bitch . . .
Ah no! he wouldn't use that phrase
To designate my mother:
Despite his high and mighty ways,
My Boss is *my twin-brother*.

Conceived were we in common joy
And born in common pain;
But while I was a brawny boy
My brother stole my brain.
As dumb was I as he was smart,
As blind as he could see;
And so it was, bang from the start
He got the best of me.

I'm one of many in his pay;
From him I draw my dough;
But he would fire me right away
If he should hap to know
A week ago he passed me by;
I heard his wheezing breath,
And in his pouched and blood-shot eye
I saw, stark-staring—Death.

He has his women, cards and wine;
I have my beans and bread.
But oh, the last laugh will be mine
The day I hear he's dead.
Aye, though we shared a common womb
(I gloat to think of it)
Some day I'll stand beside his tomb
And loose my gob and . . . *spit*.

THE TUNNEL

Toil's a tunnel, there's no way out
For fellows the likes o' me;
A beggar wi' only a crust an' a clout
At the worst o' the worst is free;
But I work to eat, an' I eat to work;
It's always the same old round,
And I dassent fail for the day I shirk
They'll shovel me underground.

I guess God meant it to be that way,
For a man must make his bread;
I was born to bondage, to earn my pay,
To slave to the day I'm dead;
To live in a tunnel, to die in a ditch—
That's just what us fellows do;
For the poor must be makin' the rich more rich,
An' the many must serve the few.

Aye, we live in a tunnel, most o' us,
A-fearin' to lose our job;
But who has the right to gripe an' cuss
So the goblet's hot on the hob
An' I musn't be havin' the wife complain,
An' I can't let the childer fast:
So I'll toil in my tunnel an' drag my chain,
Clank! Clank! Clank! to the last.

RIPE FRUIT

Through eyelet holes I watch the crowd
Rain of confetti fling;
Their joy is lush, their laughter loud,
For Carnival is King.
Behind his chariot I pace
To earn my petty pay;
They laugh to see my monster face:
"Ripe Fruit," I hear them say.

I do not laugh: my shoulders sag;
No heart have I for glee,
Because I hold aloft a hag
Who grins enough for me;
A hideous harridan who bears
In crapulous display,
Like two grub-eaten mouldy pears
Her bubbies on a tray.

Ripe Fruit! Oh, God! It's hell to think
How I have drifted down
Through vice and dice and dope and drink
To play the sordid clown;
That I who held the golden key
To operatic fame,
Should gnaw the crust of misery
And drain the dregs of shame.

What matter! I'll get soused to-night,
And happy I will be,
To sit within a tavern bright,
A trollop on my knee. . . .
So let the crazy pipers pipe,
And let the rapture ring:
Ripe fruit am I—yea, rotten ripe,
And Carnival is King.

DRAM-SHOP DITTY

I drink my fill of foamy ale
I sing a song, I tell a tale,
I play the fiddle;
My throat is chronically dry,
Yet *savant* of a sort am I,
And Life's my riddle.

For look! I raise my arm to drink—
A voluntary act, you think
(Nay, Sir, you're grinning).
You're wrong: this stein of beer I've drained
To emptiness was pre-ordained
Since Time's beginning.

But stay! 'Tis I who err, because
Time has no birth; it always was,
It will be ever;
And trivial though my act appears,
Its repercussion down the years
Will perish never.

It will condition ages hence,
But its most urgent consequence,
You'll not deny, Sir,
Is that it should be filled again
To goad my philosophic brain,
If you will buy, Sir.

There is no great, there is no small;
Fate makes a tapestry of all,
Each stitch is needed . . .
The gods be praised! that barman chap
Manipulates his frothing tap—
My plea is heeded.

Two foaming tankards over-spill,
And soon, ah! not too soon, they will
Our thirst be slaking.
Stout lad! he does not dream that he
A page of history maybe
Is blandly making.

For Sir, it was ordained that you
Buy me a drink (or maybe two)
Since ages hoary;
And doubtless it is predestined
Our meeting shall affect in kind
Earth's Cosmic Story.

The fathomless, eternal Past,
The Future infinitely vast,
We two are linking;
So let us fitly celebrate
This moment of immortal Fate
In drinking, drinking.

But though I toss a hearty pot,
Kind stranger, do not think I'm not
For Truth a groper . . .
Another? Thanks, I won't refuse,
I am a tippler, if you choose,
But not a toper.

A nice distinction! . . . Well, life's good:
Just give me beer, rich greasy food,
And let me fiddle;
Enough of dull philosophy;
To-night we'll merry, merry be . . .
Hi-diddle-diddle.

REPTILES AND ROSES

So crystal clear it is to me
That when I die I cease to be,
All else seems sheer stupidity.

All promises of Paradise
Are wishful thinking, preacher's lies,
Dogmatic dust flung in our eyes.

Yea, *life's* immortal, swift it flows
Alike in reptile and in rose,
But as it comes, so too it goes.

Dead roses will not bloom again;
The lifeless lizard writhes in vain;
Cups shattered will not hold champagne.

Our breath is brief, and being so
Let's make our heaven here below,
And lavish kindness as we go.

For when dour Death shall close the door
There will be darkness evermore;
So let us kneel in prayer before

Each day and let our duty be
To fight that Mankind may be free . . .
There is our Immortality.

FRUSTRATION

Gazing to gold of seraph wing,
With wistful wonder in my eyes,
A blue-behinded ape, I swing
Upon the palms of Paradise.

A parakeet of gaudy hue
Upon a flame tree smugly rocks;
Oh, we're a precious pair, we two,
I gibber while the parrot squawks.

"If I had but your wings," I sigh,
How ardently would I aspire
To soar celestially high
And mingle with yon angel choir."

His beady eye is bitter hard;
Right mockingly he squints at me;
As critic might review a bard
His scorn is withering to see.

And as I beat my breast and howl,
"Poor fool," he shrills, my bliss to wreck.
So . . . so I steal behind that fowl
And grab his claw and screw his neck.

And swift his scarlet wings I tear;
Seeking to soar, with hope divine,
I frantically beat the air,
And crash to earth and—snap my spine.

Yet as I lie with shaken breaths
Of pain I watch my seraph throng. . . .
Oh, I would die a dozen deaths
Could I but sing one deathless song!

FINALITY

When I am dead I will not care
How future generations fare,
For I will be so unaware.

Though fields their slain has carpeted,
And seas be salt with tears they shed,
Not one I'll waste, for I'll be dead.

Though atom bombs in ashes lay
Their skyey cities of to-day,
With carrion lips I cannot pray.

Though ruin reigns and madness raves,
And cowering men creep back to caves,
I cannot help to dig their graves.

Though fools for knowledge delve too deep,
And wake dark demons from their sleep,
I will not have the eyes to weep.

I will not care, I cannot care,
For I will be no longer there
To share their sorrow and despair.

And nevermore my heart will bleed
When on my brain the blind-worms feed,
For I'll be dead, *dead*, DEAD indeed.

And when I rot and cease to be,
It matters not a jot to me
What may be man's dark destiny.

Ah! there you have the hell of it,
As in the face of Fate I spit
I know she doesn't mind a bit.

A thousand millions clot this earth,
And billions more await their birth—
For what? . . . *Ye gods, enjoy your mirth!*

FORTITUDE

Time, the Jester, jeers at you;
Your life's a fleeting breath;
Your birth's a flimsy I.O.U.
To that old devil, Death.
And though to glory you attain,
Or be to beauty born,
Your pomp and vanity are vain:
Time ticks you off with scorn.

Time, the Cynic, sneers at you,
And stays you in your stride;
He flouts the daring deeds you do,
And pillories your pride.
The triumph of your yesterday
He pages with the Past;
He taunts you with the grave's decay
And calls the score at last.

All this I know, yet what care I!
Despite his dusty word,
I hold my tattered banner high,
And swing my broken sword.
In blackest night I glimpse a gleam,
And nurse a faith sublime,
To do, to dare, to hope, to dream,
To fight you, Foeman Time;
Yea, in the dark a deathless beam
To smite you, Tyrant Time.

GOD'S BATTLE-GROUND

God dwells in you; in pride and shame,
In all you do to blight or bless;
In all you are of praise or blame,
In beauty or in ugliness.
"Divine Creation"—What a fraud!
God did not make you . . . *You make God.*

God lives in me, in all I feel
Of love and hate, of joy and pain,
Of grace and greed, of woe and weal,
Of fear and cheer, of loss and gain:
For good or evil I am He,
Yea, saint or devil, One are we.

God fends and fights in each of us;
His altars we, or bright or dim;
So with no sacerdotal fuss
But worthy act let's worship Him:
Goodness is Godness—let us be
Deserving of Divinity.

And of His presence be aware,
And by our best His love express;
A gentle word is like a prayer,
A kindly act is holiness:
Don't let God down; let Him prevail
And write his AMEN to our tale.

SUCCESS

You ask me what I call Success—
Is it, I wonder, Happiness?

It is not wealth, it is not fame,
Nor rank nor power nor honoured name.
It is not triumph in the Arts—
Best-selling books or leading parts.
It is not plaudits of the crowd,
The flame of flags, processions proud.
The panegyrics of the Press
Are but the mirage of Success.
You may have all of them, my friend,
Yet be a failure in the end.

I've known proud Presidents of banks
Who've fought their way up from the ranks,
And party leaders of renown
Who played as boys in Shantytown.
Strong, self-made men, yet seek to trace
Benignity in any face;
Grim purpose, mastery maybe,
Yet never sweet serenity;
Never contentment, thoughts that bless—
That mellow joy *I* deem Success.

Then haply seek some humble hearth,
Quite poor in goods yet rich in mirth,
And see a man of common clay
Watching his little ones at play;
A laughing fellow full of cheer,
Health, strength and faith that mocks at fear:
Who for his happiness relies
On joys he lights in other eyes;
He loves his home and envies none. . . .
Who happier beneath the sun?

Aye, though he walk in lowly ways,
Shining Success has crowned his days.

AGNOSTIC APOLOGY

I am a stout materialist;
With abstract terms I can't agree,
And so I've made a little list
Of words that don't make sense to me.
To fool my reason I refuse,
For honest thinking is my goal;
And that is why I rarely use
      Vague words like *Soul*.

In terms of matter I am sure
This world of ours can be defined;
And so with theories obscure
I will not mystify my mind;
And though I use it more or less,
Describing alcoholic scenes,
I do not know, I must confess,
      What *Spirit* means.

When I survey this cosmic scene,
The term "Creator" seems absurd;
The Universe has always been,
Creation *never* has occurred.
But in my Lexicon of Doubt
It strikes me definitely odd,
One word I never dare to flout,
One syllable the mountains shout,
Three letters that the stars spell out:
      GOD.

REGRET

It's not for laws I've broken
That bitter tears I've wept,
But solemn vows I've spoken
And promises unkept;
It's not for sins committed
My heart is full of rue,
But gentle acts omitted,
Kind deeds I did not do.

I have outlived the blindness,
The selfishness of youth;
The canker of unkindness,
The cruelty of truth;
The searing hurt of rudeness . . .
By mercies great and small,
I've come to reckon goodness
The greatest gift of all.

Let us be helpful ever
To those who are in need,
And each new day endeavour
To do some gentle deed;
For faults beyond our grieving,
With kindliness atone;
On earth by love achieving
A Heaven of our own.

ROSY-KINS

As home from church we two did plod,
"Grandpa," said Rosy, "What is God?"
Seeking an answer to her mind,
This is the best that I could find. . . .

God is the Iz-ness of the Is,
The One-ness of our Cosmic Biz;
The high, the low, the near, the far,
The atom and the evening star;
The lark, the shark, the cloud, the clod,
The whole darned Universe—that's God.

Some deem that other gods there be,
And to them humbly bend the knee;
To Mumbo Jumbo and to Joss,
To Bud and Allah—but the Boss
Is mine . . . While there are suns and seas
My timeless God shall dwell in these.

In every glowing leaf He lives;
When roses die His life he gives;
God is not outside and apart
From Nature, but her very heart;
No Architect (as I of verse)
He is Himself the Universe.

Said Rosy-kins: "Grandpa, how odd
Is your imagining of God.
To me he's always just appeared
A huge Grandfather with a beard.

PRAYER

You talk o' prayer an' such—
Well, I jest don't know how;
I guess I got as much
Religion as a cow.
I fight an' drink an' swear;
Red hell I often raise,
But never said a prayer
    In all my days.

I'm honest, right enough;
Don't take no stock in crimes;
I'm jest a dockside tough,
An' yet . . . an' yet sometimes,
If I should happen by
A church-door open wide
The chances are that I
    Will sneak inside.

It's kind o' peaceful there,
Jest sittin' in a pew;
There's sompin' in the air
That rests me through an' through;
It does me heaps o' good
To see them candles glow,
So soothin' to the mood . . .
    Why?—I don't know.

153

Unless that sittin' still
Can be a kind o' prayer;
My heart jest seems to fill
Wi' peace . . . Oh, God don't care
For guys the likes o' me;
I just ain't in His line:
But when the CROSS I see,
I make the sign.

SILENCE

When I was cub reporter I
Would interview the Great,
And sometimes they would make reply,
And sometimes hesitate;
But often they would sharply say,
With bushy eyebrows bent:
"Young man, your answer for to-day
        Is—No Comment."

Nigh sixty years have called the tune,
And silver is my pate;
No longer do I importune
Important men of state;
But time has made me wise, and so
When button-holed I shake
My head and say: "To-day I've no
        Comment to make."

Oh, Silence is a mighty shield,
Verbosity is vain;
Let others wordy warfare wield,
From argument abstain,
When faced with dialectic foes
Just shrug and turn away:
Be sure your wisest words are those
        You do not say.

Yea, Silence is a gleaming sword
Whose wounds are hard to heal;
Its quiet stuns the spoken word
More than a thunder peal;
Against it there is no defence,
For like the grave-yard sod
Its hush is Heaven's eloquence,
    The VOICE OF GOD.

REMORSE

That scathing word I used in scorn
(Though half a century ago)
Comes back to me this April morn,
Like boomerang to work me woe;
Comes back to me with bitter blame
(Though apple boughs are blossoming),
And oh! the anguish of my shame
Is sharper than a serpent's sting!

Age sensitizes us to pain,
And when remembrance of some word
We spoke in wrath returns again,
Its stab is like a driven sword. . . .
And if in some celestial span
Our hearts in penitence may bleed
For all the hurt we've done to man—
Ah, that would be a hell indeed!

So friends, be careful of your words,
Though other breasts may meet their steel,
Lest they return like vengeful swords,
Till *yours* the wounds that never heal.
For Age the heart to mercy mellows;
Foul memories haunt like evil elves:
Let us be gentle to our fellows,
And win God's mercy for ourselves.

THE UNDYING

She was so wonderful I wondered
If wedding me she had not blundered;
She was so pure, so high above me,
I marvelled how she came to love me:
Or did she? Well, in her own fashion—
Affection, pity, never passion.

I knew I was not worth her love;
Yet oh, how wistfully I strove
To be her equal in some way;
She knew I tried, and I would pray
Some day she'd hold her head in pride,
And stand with praising by my side.

A weakling, I—she made me strong;
My finest thoughts to her belong;
Through twenty years she mothered me,
And then one day she smothered me
With kisses, saying wild with joy:
"Soon we'll be three—let's hope, a boy."

"Too old to bear a child," they said;
Well, they were right, for both are dead. . . .
Ah no, not *dead*—she is with me,
And by my side she'll ever be;
Her spirit lingers, half divine:
All good I do is hers, not mine.

God, by my works O let me strive
To keep her gentleness alive!
Let in my heart her spirit glow,
And by my thought for others show
She is not dead: she'll never die
While love for humankind have I.

YOUR POEM

My poem may be yours indeed
In melody and tone,
If in its rhythm you can read
A music of your own;
If in its pale woof you can weave
Your lovelier design,
'Twill make my lyric, I believe,
More yours than mine.

I'm but a prompter at the best;
Crude cues are all I give.
In simple stanzas I suggest—
'Tis you who make them live.
My bit of rhyme is but a frame,
And if my lines you quote,
I think, although they bear my name,
'Tis you who wrote.

Yours is the beauty that you see
In any words I sing;
The magic and the melody
'Tis you, dear friend, who bring.
Yea, by the glory and the gleam,
The loveliness that lures
Your thought to starry heights of dream,
The poem's yours.

AN OLD STORY

(RETOLD IN RHYME)

They threw him in a prison cell;
He moaned upon his bed,
And when he crept from coils of hell:
"Last night you killed," they said.

"Last night in drunken rage you slew
A being brave with breath;
A radiant soul, because of you,
Lies dark in death."

"Last night I killed," he moaned distraught,
"When I was wild with wine;
I slew, and I remember naught . . .
O Mother, Mother mine!

"To what unbridled rage may lead
You taught me at your knee.
Why did I not your warning heed . . .
And now—the gallows tree.

"O Mother, Mother, come to me,
For I am sore distrest,
And I would kneel beside your knee
And weep upon your breast. . . ."

They stared at him; their lips were dumb,
Their eyes tear-filled;
Then spoke the Priest: "She cannot come . . .
'Twas she you killed."

WHY?

He was our leader and our guide;
He was our saviour and our star.
We walked in friendship by his side,
Yet set him where our heroes are.

He taught disdain of fame and wealth;
With courage he inspired our youth;
He preached the purity of health,
And held aloft the torch of truth.

He bade us battle for the Right,
And led us in the carnage grim;
He was to us a living light,
And like a God we worshipped him.

He raised us from the grievous gloom,
And brimmed our hearts with radiant cheer;
And then he climbed up to his room,
And . . . cut his throat from ear to ear.

Let us not judge his seeming lapse;
His secret soul we could not see;
He smiled and left us, and perhaps
Death was his crowning victory.

THE LAST SUPPER

Marie Vaux of the Painted Lips
And the mouth so mocking gay,
A wanton you to the finger-tips,
Who break men's hearts in play;
A thing of dust I have striven for,
Honour and manhood given for,
Headlong to ruin driven for,
And this is the last, you say. . . .

Drinking your wine with dainty sips,
Marie Vaux of the Painted Lips.

Marie Vaux of the Painted Lips,
Long have you held your sway;
I have laughed at your merry quips—
Now is my time to pay.
What we sow we must reap again;
When we laugh we must weep again;
So to-night we will sleep again,
Nor wake until Judgement Day. . . .

'Tis a poisoned wine that your palate sips,
Marie Vaux of the Painted Lips.

Marie Vaux of the Painted Lips,
Down on your knees and pray;
Pray your last ere the moment slips,
Pray ere the dark and the terror grips,
And the bright world fades away.
Pray for the good unguessed of us,
Pray for the peace and rest of us:
Here comes the Shape in quest of us,
Now we must go away. . . .

You and I in the grave's eclipse,
Marie Vaux of the Painted Lips.

*NO NECK-TIE PARTY

A prisoner speaks:

Majority of twenty-three,
I face the Judge with joy and glee;
For am I not a lucky chap—
No more hanging, no black cap;
A "lifer", yes, but well I know
In fifteen years they'll let me go;
For I'll be pious in my prison,
Sing with gusto: Christ Is Risen;
Serve the hymn-books out on Sunday,
Sweep the chapel clean on Monday:
Such a model lag I'll be
In fifteen years they'll set me free.

Majority of twenty-three,
You've helped me cheat the gallows tree.
I'm twenty now, at thirty-five
How I will laugh to be alive!
To leap into the world again
And bless the fools miscalled "humane",
Who say the gibbet's wrong and so
At thirty-five they let me go,

---

* By a majority of twenty-three the House of Commons voted the abolition of the death penalty.

That I may sail across the sea,
A killer unsuspect and free,
To change my name, to darkly thrive
By hook or crook at thirty-five.

O silent dark and beastly wood
Where with my bloodied hands I stood!
O piteous child I raped and slew!
Had she been *yours*, would you and you
Have pardoned me and set me free,
Majority of twenty-three?
Yet by your solemn vote you willed
I shall not die though I have killed;
Although I did no mercy show,
In mercy you will let me go. . . .
That he who kills and does not pay
May live to kill another day.

CASINO CALYPSO

Although of gold I am not rich in,
And have of jewels none at all,
I'm dreaming in what's called the Kitchen
Of earth's most famous gambling hall.
I linger in a lonely corner,
And though the croupier entreats,
Of Lady Luck I am a scorner:
    I'm reading Keats.

The plunging players pack the tables,
Beneath the bunched electric's glare;
The tumult is the Tower of Babel's,
As strong as Camembert the air.
The counters click, the balls are spinning,
The number eight three times repeats—
There was a fortune for my winning:
    What price John Keats?

Yet (in parenthesis) it's funny
That I, of this gain-goaded throng,
Alone should mock the might of money,
And lose myself in golden song.
I wonder which of us is crazy,
I, toying with my rhymed conceits,
Or they, the mob with eyes greed-glazy—
    Enlight me, Keats.

Your little book of limp green leather
I sadly fear that I profane,
Because we two are linked together
In this rococo hall of gain;
That I a piddling poetaster,
A nuzzler of the muse's teats,
Should in this *milieu* con the Master—
        Forgive me, Keats.

Well, supper calls, I must be going
To whirl spaghetti from a plate;
But on my way behold I'm throwing
A louis on my number, *eight*. . . .
By gad! I've won, I've made a killing;
I'll dine on pheasant, fruit and sweets,
And golden Asti I'll be spilling
To your sweet memory, God willing,
        Divine John Keats:
Aye, fluted glasses I'll be filling
        To toast you, Keats.

RIVIERA HONEYMOON

Beneath the trees I lounged at ease
And watched them speed the pace;
They swerved and swung, they clutched and clung,
They leapt in roaring chase;
The crowd was thrilled, a chap was killed:
It was a splendid race.

Two men, they say, went West that day,
But I knew only one;
Geranium-red his blood was spread
And blazoned in the sun;
A lightning crash . . . Lo! in a flash
His racing days were done.

I did not see—such sights to me
Appallingly are grim;
But for a girl of sunny curl
I would not mention him,
That English lad with grin so glad,
And racing togs so trim.

His motor bike was painted like
A postal box of red,
'Twas gay to view . . . "We bought it new,"
A voice beside me said.
"Our little bit we blew on it
The day that we were wed.

"We took a chance: through sunny France
We flashed with flaunting power.
With happy smiles a hundred miles
Or more we made an hour.
Like flame we hurled into a world
A-foam with fruit and flower.

"Our means were small; we risked them all
This famous race to win,
So we can take a shop and make
Our bread—one must begin.
We're not afraid; Jack has his trade:
He's bright as brassy pin.

"Hark! Here they come; uphill they hum;
My lad has second place;
They swing, they roar, they pass once more,
Now Jack sprints up the pace.
They're whizzing past . . . At last, at last
He leads—he'll *win* the race.

"Another round . . . They leap, they bound,
But—where O where is he?"
And then the girl with sunny curl
Turned chalk-faced unto me,
Within her eyes a wild surmise
It was not good to see.

They say like thunder-bolt he crashed
Into a wall of stone;
To bloody muck his face was mashed,
He died without a moan:
In borrowed black the girl went back
To London Town alone.

Beneath the trees I lounged at ease
And saw them pep the pace;
They swerved and swung, they clutched and clung
And roaring was the chase:
Two men, they say, were croaked that day—
It was a glorious race.

WRESTLING MATCH

What guts he had, the Dago lad
Who fought that Frenchman grim with guile;
For nigh an hour they milled like mad,
And mauled the mat in rare old style.
Then up and launched like catapaults,
And tangled, twisted, clinched and clung,
Then tossed in savage somersaults,
And hacked and hammered, ducked and swung;
And groaned and grunted, sighed and cried,
Now knotted tight, now springing free;
To bend each other's bones they tried,
Their faces crisped in agony. . . .

Then as rage rose, with tiger-bound,
They clashed and smashed, and flailed and flung,
And tripped and slipped, with hammer-pound,
And streaming sweat and straining lung.
The mighty mob roared out their joy,
And wild I heard a wench near-by
Shriek to the Frenchman: "Atta Boy!
Go to it, Jo-jo—kill the guy."

The boy from Rome was straight and slim,
And swift and springy as a bow;
The man from Metz was gaunt and grim,
But all the tricks he seemed to know.

'Twixt knee and calf with scissors-lock,
He gripped the lad's arm like a vice;
The prisoned hand went white as chalk,
And limp as death and cold as ice.
And then he tried to break the wrist,
And kidney-pounded with his knee,
But with a cry and lightning twist
The Roman youth had wrested free. . . .

Then like mad bulls they hooked and mauled,
And blindly butted, bone on bone;
Spread-eagled on the mat they sprawled,
And writhed and rocked with bitter moan.
Then faltered to their feet and hung
Upon the ropes with eyes of woe;
And then the Frenchman stooped and flung
The wop among the mob below,
Who helped to hoist him back again,
With cheers and jeers and coarse cat-calls,
To where the Gaul with might and main
Hung poised to kick his genitals
And drop him senseless in the ring. . . .
And then an old man cried: "My son!"
The maddened mob began to fling
Their chairs about—the fight was done.

Soft silver sandals tapped the sea;
Palms listened to the lack of sound;

The lucioles were lilting free,
The peace was precious and profound.
Oh had it been an evil dream? . . .
A chapel of the Saints I sought,
And there before the altar gleam
I clasped my hands and thought and thought. . . .

SOLDIER BOY

My soldier boy has crossed the sea
    To fight the foeman;
But he'll come back to make of me
    An honest woman.
So I am singing all day long,
    Despite blood-shedding;
For though I know he's done me wrong,
    We'll end by wedding.

My soldier boy is home again,
    So bold and scathless;
But oh, my heart is numb with pain
    Because he's faithless.
He's brought with him a French Mam'selle;
    They plan a marriage;
Maybe I'll go—no one will know
    Of my miscarriage.

My soldier boy has made his choice,
    She'll hold him to it;
I tell myself that I rejoice,
    May he not rue it.
But oh, that starry month of May,
    Love-words wild spoken!
I stand alone and make no moan . . .
    My heart is broken.

VILLAGE VIRTUE

Jenny was my first sweetheart;
Poor lass! she was none too smart.
Though I swore she'd never rue it,
She would never let me do it.
When I tried she made a fuss,
So damn pure and virtuous.
Girls should cozen all they can,
Use their wiles to get their man.

June, my second, was no prude;
Too good-looking to be good;
Wanton and a giddy-gadder,
Never knew who might have had her;
Kept me mad and jumping jealous,
Tempting all the other fellows
Like a wayside flower to pluck her:
So at last I had to chuck her.

Now I'm settled down with Jill,
And we're safely married still.
She began to wail and worry,
So we wedded in a hurry.
Well, it's quite all right that way—
We're all made of common clay,
And the grey-haired folk that bore us
Just as wanton were before us.

June, I hear, now lives in London
Where, I fear, she's sadly undone.
Jenny, still as virtuous
Missed the matrimonial bus.
Where our "first" set gossips buzzin'
Jill and I now have a dozen,
Ready in their turn to prove
There's no chastity in love.

June, so fickle and so fair,
Common was as barber's chair;
Jill provides me with good grub.
Lets me go nights to the pub.
Though her silver hairs are many.
One eve I might call on Jenny . . .
She may not need too much urging:
Must be hell to die a virgin.

M

VILLAGE DON JUAN

Lord, I'm grey, my race is run,
But by old Harry, I've had my fun;
And all about, I seem to see
Lads and lassies that look like me;
Ice-blue eyes on every hand,
Handsomest youngsters in the land.

"Old Stud Horse" they say of me,
But back of my beard I laugh with glee.
Far and wide have I sown my seed,
Yet by the gods I've improved the breed:
From byre and stable to joiner's bench,
From landlord's daughter to serving wench.

Ice-blue eyes and blade-straight nose,
Stamp of my virile youth are those;
Now you'll see them on every side,
Proof of my prowess, far and wide:
Even the Parson's handsome scamp,
And the Doctor's daughter have my stamp.

Many a matron cocks an eye
Of secret knowledge as I pass by;
As for the hubbies, what they don't know
Will never hurt them, so let them go:
The offspring most they seem to prize
Have blade-straight noses and ice-blue eyes.

Yet oh, I have a haunting dread
Brother and sister lust and bed;
The Parson's son and the Doctor's lass,
Yestreen in the moon I saw them pass;
The thought of them wed is like a knife. . . .
Brother and sister—man and wife.

DEATH AND LIFE

'Twas in the grave-yard's gruesome gloom
That May and I were mated;
We sneaked inside and on a tomb
Our love we consummated.
It's quite all right, no doubt we'll wed,
Our sin will go unchidden . . .
Ah! sweeter than the nuptial bed
Are ecstasies forbidden.

And as I held my sweetheart close,
And she was softly sighing,
I could not help but think of those
In peace below us lying.
Poor folks! No disrespect we meant,
And begs you'll be forgiving;
We hopes the dead will not resent
The rapture of the living.

And when in death I, too, shall lie,
And lost to those who love me,
I wish two sweethearts roving by
Will plight their troth above me.
Oh do not think that I will grieve
To hear the vows they're voicing,
And if their love new life conceive,
'Tis I will be rejoicing.

RESOLUTIONS

Each New Year's Eve I used to brood
On my misdoings of the past,
And vowed: "This year I'll be so good—
Well, haply better than the last."
My record of reforms I read
To Mum who listened sweetly to it:
"Why *plan* all this, my son?" she said;
  "Just do it."

Of her wise words I've often thought—
Aye, sometimes with a pang of pain,
When resolutions come to naught,
And high resolves are sadly vain;
The human heart from failure bleeds;
Hopes may be wrecked so that we rue them . . .
Don't let us dream of lovely deeds—
  Just do them.

And so, my son, uphold your pride.
Believe serenely in your soul.
Just take things in a steady stride,
Until behold! you've gained your goal.
But if, perchance, you frame a plan
Of conduct, let it be a free one:
Don't try to *make* yourself a man—
  Just *be* one.

181

STRIVING

Striving is life, yet life is striving;
I fight to live, yet live to fight;
The vital urge is in me driving,
Yet I must drive with all my might:
Each day a battle, and the fray
Stoutly renewed the coming day.

I am myself—yet when I strive
I build a self that's truer, higher;
I keep my bit of God alive
And forge me in heroic fire:
What if my goal I never gain—
Better to toil than to attain.

It is not what I do or make,
It is the travail of my trying;
The aim, the effort and the ache
Is in the end my glorifying:
Though triumph I may never see,
The will to win is victory.

Striving is strength: with all that's in me
I will not falter in the fray;
And though no shining crown it win me,
I'll fight unto my latest day:
Strive on!—and though I win no place,
Uphold the spirit of the race.

Behold yon peaks that mock my climbing. . . .
I peer from out the dusty plain;
Dark falls, the mission bells are chiming
As on to starry heights I strain;
Despite the night up, up I plod
To gain the golden meads of God.

AN OLIVE FIRE

An olive fire's a lovely thing;
Somehow it makes me think of Spring
As in my grate it over-spills
With dancing flames like daffodils.
They flirt and frolic, twist and twine,
The brassy fire-irons wink and shine. . . .
Leap gold, you flamelets! Laugh and sing:
An olive fire's a lovely thing.

An olive fire's a household shrine:
A crusty loaf, a jug of wine,
An apple and a chunk of cheese—
Oh I could be content with these.
But if my cruse of oil is there,
To fry a fresh-caught fish, I swear
I do not envy any king,
As sitting by my hearth I sing:
An olive fire's a lovely thing.

When old and worn, of life I tire,
I'll sit before an olive fire,
And watch the feather ash like snow
As softly as a rose heart glow;
The tawny roots will loose their hoard
Of sunbeams centuries have stored,
And flames like yellow chickens cheep,
Till in my heart Peace is so deep:
With hands prayer-clasped I sleep . . . and sleep.

MY INDIAN SUMMER

Here in the Autumn of my days
My life is mellowed in a haze.
Unpleasant sights are none too clear,
Discordant sounds I hardly hear.
Infirmities like buffers soft
Sustain me tranquilly aloft.
I'm deaf to duffers, blind to bores,
Peace seems to percolate my pores.
I fold my hands, keep quiet mind,
In dogs and children joy I find.
With temper tolerant and mild,
Myself you'd almost think a child.
Yea, I have come on pleasant ways
Here in the Autumn of my days.

Here in the Autumn of my days
I can allow myself to laze,
To rest and give myself to dreams:
Life never was so sweet, it seems.
I haven't lost my sense of smell,
My taste-buds never served so well.
I love to eat delicious food
Has never seemed one half so good.
In tea and coffee I delight,
I smoke and sip my grog at night.

I have a softer sense of touch,
For comfort I enjoy so much.
My skies are far more blues than greys,
Here in the Autumn of my days.

Here in the Autumn of my days
My heart is full of peace and praise.
Yet though I know that Winter's near,
I'll meet and greet it with a cheer.
With friendly books, with cosy fires,
And few but favourite desires,
I'll live from strife and woe apart,
And make a Heaven in my heart.
For Goodness, I have learned, is best,
And should by Kindness be expressed.
And so December with a smile
I'll wait and welcome, but meanwhile,
Blest interlude! The Gods I praise,
For this, the Autumn of my days.

ADVENTURE

Out of the wood my White Knight came:
His eyes were bright with a bitter flame,
As I clung to his stirrup leather;
For I was only a dreaming lad,
Yet oh, what a wonderful faith I had!
And the song in my heart was never so glad,
As we took to the trail together.

"Friends and lovers, good-bye," I said;
Never once did I turn my head,
Though wickedly wild the weather.
Mine were the rover's rags and scars,
And the rover's bed beneath the stars,
But never the shadow of prison bars,
As we ranged the world together.

Dreary and darkling was the trail,
But my Knight was clad in a gleaming mail,
And he plucked from his plume a feather.
And oh how foolishly proud was I!
"I'll wear it," I told him, "till I die;
Freemen we'll be of sea and sky,
To the ends of the earth together."

*　　*　　*　　*　　*

Yet now I know by my failing breath
I'm ripe for the last adventure, Death,
And I've reached the end of my tether:
But my Knight of the shining mail is there,
And his eyes are bright and he bids me dare:
So into the Dark let's boldly fare,
Into the Dark . . . together.

ROSE LEAVES

When they shall close my careless eyes
And look their last upon my face,
I fear that some will say: "Here lies
    A man of deep disgrace;
His thoughts were bare, his words were brittle,
He dreamed so much, he did so little."

When they shall seal my coffin lid
And this worn mask I know as ME,
Shall from the sight of man be hid
    To all eternity—
Some one may say: "His sins were many.
His virtues—really, had he any?"

When I shall lie beneath my tomb,
Oh do not grave it with my name,
But let one rose-bush o'er me bloom,
    And heedless of my shame,
With velvet shade and loving laugh,
In petals write my epitaph.

LAST LOOK

What would I choose to see when I
To this bright earth shall bid good-bye?
When fades forever from my sight
The world I've loved with long delight?
What would I pray to look on last,
When Death shall draw the Curtain fast?

I've loved the farewell of the Sun,
Low-lapsing after work well done;
Or leaping from a sea forlorn,
Gold-glad to greet a day new born. . . .
Shall I elect to round my dream
The Sun I hail as Lord Supreme?

Ah no! Of Heaven's shining host,
It is the Moon I love the most;
And if, when I shall cease to be,
God let's me keep one memory
Of loveliness that held me thrall,
The Moon's the one I would recall.

. . . *The new Moon fine as pearly clip*
From Cleopatra's finger-tip;
The ripe Moon vaulting o'er the trees
As ruddy as a Cheddar cheese;
. . . *The late Moon, frail and wanly fair,*
Relaxed on silver rocking chair. . . .

But most of all, the Moon intense
With radiant indifference;
So placid, glacid, pure, serene,
Of all perfection proudly Queen. . . .
O Mistress Mine, let me adore
Your beauty but one moment more!
One last look . . . Let the Curtain fall,
Then let me look no more at all.

THE END OF THE TRAIL

Life, you've been mighty good to me,
Yet here's the end of the trail;
No more mountain, moor and sea,
No more saddle and sail.
Waves a-leap in the laughing sun
Call to me as of yore. . . .
Alas! my errant days are done:
I'll rove no more, no more.

Life, you've cheered me all the way;
You've been my bosom friend;
But gayest dog will have his day,
And biggest binge must end.
Shorebound I watch and see afar
A wistful isle grow wan,
While over it a last lone star
Dims out in lilac dawn.

Life, you've been wonderful to me,
But fleetest foot must fail;
The hour must come when all will see
The last lap of the trail.
Yet holding in my heart a hymn
Of praise for gladness gone,
Serene I wait *my* star to dim
In the glow of the Greater Dawn.

FINALE

Here in this vale of sweet abiding,
My ultimate and dulcet home,
That gently dreams above the chiding
Of restless and impatient foam;
Beyond the hazards of hell weather,
The harceling of wind and sea,
With timbers morticed tight together
My old hulk havens happily.

The dawn exultantly discloses
My lawn lit with mimosa gold;
The joy of January roses
Is with me when rich lands are cold;
Serene with bells of beauty chiming,
This dream domain to me belongs,
By sweet conspiracy of rhyming,
And virtue of some idle songs.

I thank the gracious Lord of Living
Who gave me power and will to write:
May I be worthy of His giving
And win to merit in His sight. . . .
O merciful and mighty Master,
Though I have faltered in the past,
Your scribe I be. . . . Despite disaster
Let me be faithful to the last.

Provence, 1949